Molly's First *Golden* Year

Alma F Quick

Charlie Dawg

Press

Acknowledgments

I wish to thank the following people for their contributions to this book:

For early readings, editing and comments – my mom, Mabel Harris, my children, Diane Bessenbacher, Elaine Jacques, Sherry Savorelli, Mark Sherwood and Donald Sherwood, my sister-in-law, Ellen Morris, and Rev. Carla McClellan.

Thank you to my first writing group, the YaYas - Christa Minks-Brown, Donna Drake, Cheryl Hays, Diana Stoppelmoor and Shirley Williams.

I am forever indebted to Michael Humphrey (it wouldn't have happened without him) for his wisdom, guidance, patience and encouragement and to the other members of the West Bottoms critique group–Judy Crotchett, Janet Dutton and Marie Wakefield.

To the Plaza critique group, also led by Michael Humphrey - Judy Crotchett, Janet Dutton, Anna Egli-Maynard, Cay Heiman, Violet Huey, Judy Kirkpatrick and Diana Stoppelmoor, and to the memory of our beloved Margaret Dart; Val Conder and Vicki Erwin, fellow participants in the 2010 Nebraska Summer Writer's Conference workshop and Harley Jane Kozak for her invaluable assistance and encouragement in that workshop; Dr. John W. Collins, Jr. for generously taking the time to answer my long list of questions, and to his nurse, Bonnie Cowan, for arranging the meeting with him; Reverend Dale Worley, "holy honky-tonk" piano player; A nod to Nancy McClelland for a great line; Ken at First Editing; And finally, my darlin', C.F. Dorrell, for a place to do revisions beside the woods at his peaceful Missouri Ozarks home.

Dedication

I dedicate this book to the memory of my amazing, indomitable mom, Mabel Harris, who always believed I could do it — even when I wasn't sure.

Chapter 1

Molly nearly poked her eye out with her mascara wand when she heard her name on the radio.

"And now," said the morning deejay, "it's time for a shout out to Molly Stark, retiring today after 25 years at Heartland Distributing. Congratulations, Molly. Here's to the first day of your golden years."

Next, Johnny Paycheck sang the line, "Take this job and shove it."

Wonder which one of my staff arranged that, Molly thought. *Most likely it was a rare case of teamwork.*

A moment later the deejay said, "Hi, caller, you're on the air."

A querulous voice shouted, "Golden years, my ass."

"Excuse me," the deejay said. "Are you calling with a request?"

"I'm calling," the peevish voice continued, "to tell Molly-what's-her- name that all that golden years' bull is another one of the big lies, like he'll still respect you in the morning. Well, don't you believe it, honey. What you've got to look forward to is memory loss, wrinkles, sags, chin hair, aching joints, cataracts, hemorrhoids, overactive bladder and a whole bucket load of other crap."

A long moment of dead air followed while Molly chuckled at the deejay's uncharacteristic loss for words. She studied her reflection, pulled her neck taut with her thumbs and lifted her face upward with her palms and fingers. How much would a facelift cost? How painful would it be? *Ah, hell,* she thought, relinquishing her face and neck to gravity, *I'd rather spend my money to see the world and let the world see the real me.*

Twenty minutes later, Molly was headed west toward downtown Kansas City with the April morning sun in her rearview mirror, a song in her heart and a lump in her throat, because she would never have to make this trip again.

~~

A hollow feeling of finality trailed Molly like a shadow as she went about her last day at Heartland Distributing. She had already packed most of her personal items and taken them home. Her small office echoed its emptiness. She stared out the window at the loading dock across the street, where pigeons reported for the start of their day. It wasn't the best view in the world but at least she'd had a window for the past 11 years. Not bad for someone who started out as a billing clerk earning minimum wage.

A familiar pang of grief shook her as she picked up the framed photo of Sam and wrapped it in newspaper for the trip home. Why couldn't he have lived to help her celebrate this moment?

A beep from her computer alerted Molly to an incoming message. She glanced at the sender's name and braced herself for an assault on the English language.

"From Doug Harmon, Account Manager. To who it may concern. As it pertains to All City Supply they will be on a new phone system affective immediately starting Monday. There system will be of the direct line type, so for example. If you are trying to get a holt of Will H. his extension is 242. So you would call 327-6242. All there extensions have stayed the same. If any questions as it regards this matter, dont hesitate to call myself."

Molly read the message again, and then forwarded it to the company president with a preface that read:

Sherm, I understand Doug is a hell of a salesman, but I humbly suggest you disable the letter keys on his computer.

Your faithful servant to the bitter end, Molly.

She hesitated only a split second before she hit *Send.*

Almost immediately, a reply came back:

Thanks for your input, Molly. How long have you been holding that inside? By the way, I'm going to miss you. Who will be our resident grammar Nazi after you're gone?

Sherm

There was a light tap on the door. Molly looked up to see a pretty, mocha face peek through the glass. She said, "Come in, Amy."

God, she was going to miss this girl. Not only that, she was worried about her.

Amy parked her attractive, appropriately dressed, highly efficient self in a chair in front of Molly's desk.

"Well, boss lady, it's almost over. I'm thinkin' about packin' my bags, too." Tears swam in her big, brown eyes.

Molly struggled to keep her tough face on. "You know, acting like a girl won't get you anywhere. Did you talk to Sherm again?"

"Yeah, I got a long-winded speech about how the company's growing... the days of promoting from within are a thing of the past...they're gonna be looking for men with degrees to fill the management positions from now on. He actually said *men*, Molly. Then there was some crap about the Peter Principle. What the hell is that?"

Molly felt a rush of anger at the way the world was changing around her. She said, "All you really need to know about the Peter Principle is, if you don't have one, you're screwed."

Amy nodded and sighed. "Well, damn."

The silence stretched on while Molly tried to think of some way to encourage Amy. She was sick of all the biz-speak and buzzwords that came out of the motivational seminars everyone was attending. She was sick of hearing people call something a challenge when it was obviously a problem. She remembered fondly the days when you could call a spade a fucking shovel. She was more than ready to walk away from it all.

Finally, she said, "Sorry, Amy, that wasn't helpful. I want you to go back to your computer and Google Peter Principle.

And go talk to Sherm again. Tell him you looked it up. Then tell him you want to sign up for the Quick-Steps-to-Success program."

"What does that involve? A boob job and shorter skirts?"

"No, that would be A-*Quickie*-Steps-To-Success. And if someone gets fired over it, you can bet your 401K it won't be Peter." She got up, hugged Amy and shooed her out before they both started bawling.

At noon, Molly's staff informed her they were planning to take her to lunch at The Cheesecake Factory. "All of you?" she asked. "That would mean shutting down the entire department."

"Who you gonna leave behind?" her catalog designer asked. Molly looked at five eager faces.

"No one," she said. "If there's a problem, I'll take the blame. They can fire me if they don't like it."

~~

After lunch, Molly spent the rest of the afternoon putting the finishing touches on a packet for Amy. It was a carefully thought out proposal for Amy to present to Sherm, as if it were her idea. It included information about the company's Quick-Steps-To-Success program, a list of classes and training seminars, how to ask the company to pay for them, and how each one would further Amy's value to the company. Molly's last official act was to call Amy into her office and go over the packet with her.

"Tell him this is your five-year plan and you'd like to get started on it as soon as you've shown the new marketing manager the ropes and helped him ease into the position."

"Wow, that sounds kind of pushy. I don't know if I can pull it off." "Yes, you can. Practice in front of a mirror until you can say it with a straight face."

Amy picked up the packet and stood. "Oh, Molly, I'm gonna—"

Molly held up her hand to interrupt Amy's words. "Scram," she said. "I'll see you at the party."

4

At 5 o'clock, Molly turned off her computer one final time. Across the street, the pigeons had left for the day. She closed her office door and went to join her co-workers, customers and vendors for her retirement party.

I hope they got me a male stripper instead of Waterford crystal, she thought.

Chapter 2

It was the middle of the following week. Molly sat at the kitchen table and regarded her to-do list. Nothing had been marked off.

She had slept late and awakened disoriented from a strange dream. It was one of those dreams that left the residue of a feeling but when she tried to remember details, they stayed just out of reach. She closed her eyes and concentrated, chasing the fragments. It wasn't unusual for her to have sexual dreams; she thought of them as the female equivalent of a wet dream and Sam was always her co-star. But this one was different. It had felt dangerous. The man who was causing her arousal was a stranger.

She shook off the dream, picked up the phone and dialed her daughter. "Hi, Mom," Sophie answered. "How's retirement?"

"I'm trying to get started on my to-do list. I need a recent 8x10 of you and Myron — or a family picture of you two with the boys. And how come this year's school pictures of the kids are just 5x7s?"

"Mom, how come you just now noticed? You haven't changed the pictures on your wall for three years, so I figured the 8x10s were wasted on you. Myron's mom changes them the very day she gets them."

Molly chewed on that for a moment. "I'm sure I can't compete with the grandmother of the year, but I'm trying to do better. That's why I'm calling."

"Okay, Mom. Don't get in a snit. And don't go getting all grandmotherly on me. Myron's mom also wears orthopedic shoes and bibbed aprons. The boys won't know what to think if you stop coloring your hair and painting your toenails."

After she hung up from talking to Sophie, Molly made another call. "Liz," she said to the voice on the other end, "are you going to be home? I need a best friend fix."

Liz's daughter was leaving with her children as Molly arrived at Liz's house. She held a squirming toddler in one arm and turned loose of a hyper 3-year-old to hug Molly with the other.

"Hey, Molly, I'd like to stay and visit, but I have to run. You and Mom try to stay out of trouble," she said.

"Honey, your mom and I haven't been in serious trouble since eighth grade," Molly answered, removing the toddler's sticky hand from her hair.

Liz held the door open, shaking her head. "I think she gets a kick out of imagining us getting into trouble. I find it a little condescending."

"Oh, I don't know," Molly said, as she and Liz blazed a trail through two hours' worth of toddler devastation on the way to the kitchen. "Remember when we were 15 and went to Emery-Bird's and tried on maternity clothes to see what we'd look like when we got pregnant?"

"Yeah, we thought we looked cute. Didn't take long to dispel that notion, did it? Grab a cup of coffee while I try to restore order."

Molly surveyed the damage. Pans and Tupperware containers had been pulled from the cupboards as if the toys Liz kept for the grandchildren were not enough. A messy high chair was surrounded by a crop of Cheerios on the floor and Liz looked as if she'd just crawled out of a foxhole.

"Can I help?" Molly asked.

"No, you're not dressed for hazmat duty. Just sit."

Liz was wiping something unidentifiable off the tray of the high chair when the phone rang. She picked it up and barked, "Yeah," in her usual abrupt manner. Then, "Oh, it's you, babe," she said sweetly, as she scraped at a stubborn glob on the arm of the high chair. "Whatcha think I'm doin', big boy? I've got the house cleaned, I've just stepped out of the shower, all soft and sweet-smelling, and you know what else?" she purred into the phone as she picked up the remnants of a

7

peanut butter and jelly sandwich from the floor. "I'm thinking about you...and I'm touching myself."

There was a pause while she listened, then she cooed, "Ooh, baby. Hurry home, I'll be waiting for you." She hung up the phone.

Molly looked at her chubby friend, standing there in her shapeless shift trying to kick a sticky Cheerio off her bare foot. "I'm picturing Joe's face if he rushes home for a romantic interlude and finds you like this."

"Oh, he won't but he has stopped putting me on the speakerphone. And by the time he gets home from work, it'll all be true. The house will be clean, I'll be soft and sweet-smelling. He'll run in, wrap me in a big bear hug, smooch me up and then ask what's for dinner."

Molly laughed. She could still feel her mouth stretched in a smile when she felt tears running down her face.

Liz sat down and took Molly's hands in hers. "What's wrong, Molly?" "Oh, Liz, I hope retiring wasn't a mistake. I don't know what to do with myself. Jan keeps nagging me about traveling with her and the Halsteads and I can't work up any enthusiasm for that. In fact, I think about it with dread."

"I thought you couldn't wait to retire and see the world. And what's wrong with the Halsteads? Jan and your brother used to travel all over the world with them before Arnie died. So what's the problem?"

"It's not the way I dreamed of traveling. It was supposed to be Sam and me. I suppose I should be thrilled to take Arnie's place in this cozy little group. But it doesn't feel right." She felt the tears start again.

Liz brought a box of tissues to the table.

Molly mopped the tears away. "Liz, I'm glad you still have Joe and you guys are still in love and happy. But I'm so jealous, if you weren't my best friend, I'd hate you."

Liz squeezed Molly's hands. "I'm so sorry, Molly," she said. After a moment, she went on, "Not sorry I still have Joe. I'm sorry you don't still have Sam...or someone."

Molly looked up. "Or someone? What do you mean, *or someone?*"

"I was thinking," Liz said, "you should join one of those Internet dating services."

Chapter 3

"Molly, you have to go with us. We've got four tickets to Phantom of the Opera." It was the fourth time her sister-in-law had called in the week since Molly retired.

"I'm not taking no for an answer. It's the perfect opportunity for you to get together with the Halsteads and find out if you're a good fit for our little group."

Molly gritted her teeth. "Jan, what's in this for you? Why don't you just keep going with them like you have ever since Arnie died?"

"If you must know, sometimes I feel like a fifth wheel — or in this case a third wheel. For example, if they're sitting across a table from me, holding hands and looking all goo-goo eyed, it's uncomfortable for me. If you come on the cruise with us, you and I can strike out on our own sometimes and meet back up with them when they're through with the touchy-feely crap."

"You're an incurable romantic," Molly said.

"On a more practical note," Jan continued, "it would be nice to pay one-fourth instead of one-third when there's a cost that has to be shared. Or to pay half of my cabin on a cruise."

So that was Jan's angle — and Jan always had an angle. She wanted to save money and have someone to hang out with when Ray and Margot were tired of her.

Molly was torn between sympathy for Jan's widowhood and annoyance at the feeling of being used for her convenience. But she really would love to see Phantom of the Opera.

"Fine. How much do I owe for the ticket — and what does one wear to the, the-AY-tah?"

I hope I don't regret this she thought as she gave in. Every time she had been around them, the Halsteads had come off snooty and condescending. Not only that, Jan put on airs when she was in their presence. Oh, well, how bad could it be? A couple of hours with everyone focused on the play —she could handle that.

~~

The four of them sat around a table at a downtown restaurant after the play, and discussed it. That is, three of them discussed it. Molly felt overwhelmed by their superior knowledge of the play, the music, and the actors, whom they compared, at great length, to those who had played the same roles in other performances of the Phantom that they had seen.

"Michael Crawford was the original phantom, you know," Margot Halstead said. "I enjoyed him so much more than I did John Cudia, didn't you Ray?" Her husband and Jan both nodded sagely.

"Although," she continued, "I thought Trista Moldovan was a convincing Christine in this production."

Convincing? Molly mouthed the question to her sister-in-law as the waiter set plates of appetizers in front of them. Jan avoided Molly's eyes.

Molly wished this interminable evening was over. She hadn't counted on the extra face time with them. She was reminded again why she had never liked the Halsteads — and why she didn't like the way Jan acted around them. It seemed like they were all trying to out-snob each other. She realized Margot was speaking to her.

"Molly? Molly, what did you think?"

Molly felt as if she'd been impaled on a swizzle stick in the center of the table.

"I'm sorry," she said, "but this is the first time I've seen it. I don't know anything about the actors. But I did like the music," she finished lamely. "I'm going to look for the CD."

Margot sat there with her perfect body encased in her perfect theater attire, her slash of red mouth stretched over unnaturally white teeth in what Molly assumed was supposed to pass for a smile.

"Be sure you get the right one, the Michael Crawford version, the music of Andrew Lloyd Webber," Margot said in a tone that suggested she cared deeply. "Shall I write it down for you?"

"I know I'm culturally challenged and I have trouble keeping Andrew Lloyd Webber and Frank Lloyd Wright straight in my mind. But I'll try to remember it's the singer, not the architect, right?"

If Margot hadn't snickered and regarded Molly as if she were an interesting specimen, Molly might have stopped with that. But Margot did and Molly didn't.

"I actually thought the Cudia dude was pretty good," Molly said. "That piece at the end, 'The Music of the Night' is still running through my head. Even though I've only seen it once, and never in London or on Broadway, I'll tell you what I thought of the play — pardon me, *production* — I loved it. And one more thing, I would have stayed with the Phantom and Raoul could have crawled back into his little canoe and sailed right back where he came from."

She picked up her fork and attacked an egg roll while Margot and Ray exchanged looks, and Jan sank a little lower in her chair.

Silence descended like a final curtain call and surrounded their table.

It was so quiet Molly could hear herself chew.

Ray finally broke the tension, "So, Jan, have you read any good books lately?"

For the remainder of the meal, it seemed to Molly as if her table mates talked too brightly, smiled unnecessarily, and tried very hard to pretend they didn't notice there was a big, fat albatross hanging around their collective necks.

As they waited for the server to clear dishes and bring coffee, Molly excused herself and went to the ladies' room. She was leaning close to the mirror over the washbasin, inspecting her teeth for offending bits of food when Jan came in.

12

"That could have gone better," Jan observed dryly.

Molly met her sister-in-law's eyes in the mirror. "I'm sorry, Jan. I know you had high hopes for this to work out, but I'm pretty sure it's not going to. I think they're snooty as hell and I'm sure they think I'm a cretin. I wonder how you were ever able to mold my brother into someone the Halsteads approved of."

"You've got to be kidding. Nobody ever molded Arnie into anything. People accepted him for what he was, and they'll come to accept you, too, if you give them time."

"*They'll* come to accept *me*?" Molly blotted her lipstick on a paper towel and threw it into the receptacle. "What if *I* don't accept *them*? I'd rather be at home sorting my socks."

"Come on, Molly," Jan begged. "Just come back to the table and drink your coffee and try to be nice for 15 minutes. Then we'll go."

~~

An hour later, Jan pulled into Molly's driveway to drop her off. Molly already had her keys in her hand. "Do you want to come in?" she asked without enthusiasm.

"No," Jan said, "I'd better get home. We'll talk tomorrow, after you have a chance to regroup."

Molly kicked off her shoes at the door, threw her handbag onto the nearest chair, and peeled off her clothes on the way to the bedroom. She pulled a baggy tee shirt over her head, then returned to the living room and rummaged through her CDs until she found "George Jones' Greatest Hits." She took it to the player in her bedroom. When the familiar music started, she flopped down on the bed, closed her eyes and tried to unwind.

On the way home, she had reluctantly promised Jan she would give it another try with the Halsteads. After all, they had been nice as you please when they were parting from Molly and Jan outside the restaurant. They were all friendliness and smiles. "So nice to get to know you better,

13

Molly. We're looking forward to the cruise. Get those bags packed, blah, blah, blah."

Molly tried to tell herself maybe they weren't as bad as she was making them out to be. Maybe it was just her insecurities and the fact that this wasn't how it was supposed to turn out. Margot and Ray had each other. Jan didn't seem to miss Arnie like Molly missed Sam. Life wasn't fair, damn it.

She fell asleep with John Cudia and George Jones fighting for space inside her head.

She dreamed she was in the ship's cabin trying to get ready to go to dinner. But when she opened her suitcase, the only thing inside was a ratty terrycloth robe with a torn pocket.

Chapter 4

"Please, Mister Custer, I don't wanta go," Molly sang as she sorted laundry and tried, unsuccessfully, to imagine herself on a cruise ship with Jan and the Halsteads. Her thoughts were interrupted by the ringing of the phone.

She glanced at the caller ID. It was a long distance number she didn't recognize. "Hello?"

"Hello, Molly? This is Gil Parker."

"I'm sorry. Who?" She brushed her hair away from her ear and repositioned the phone.

"Gil Parker, Dennis's dad. I hope you don't think it's presumptuous of me to call you since we've never met."

"Not at all," Molly said. "I guess we'll be meeting soon, anyway. The wedding isn't that far off."

"That's why I'm calling," Gil said.

Oh, no, Molly thought. *Don't tell me he's not going to show up.* She waited for the bomb to drop.

"I was thinking," Gil said, "it would be nice if I could meet you before the big event. See if you and our sons have it all under control or if there's anything I can do to help."

"Wait, let me adjust the volume. I thought I just heard a father offer to help with a wedding — without being asked."

Gil laughed. "It's my excuse to come to Missouri and meet some of Richie's family before chaos descends. But I really am willing to do my part if I know what that is."

"Good luck," Molly said. I haven't been able to pin them down about anything. I've been the mother of the bride, but I don't have any idea what my role is as the mother of one of the grooms in a gay wedding. And what about you? Since you're the only father in the picture, are you going to give Dennis away? Oh, God. I hope nobody's wearing a veil."

15

"I'll try to discourage that," Gil said. "What I'd like to do is come out there and spend a few days. I plan to be in Independence on Thursday. Would it be possible for the four of us to get together sometime over the weekend?"

"I can call and set something up. Will you be staying with them?" "Oh, God, no," Gil said. "Wait. I didn't mean that to sound so harsh. I'm just afraid Dennis would try to alphabetize my shaving kit."

"I can see where you might find that annoying."

"Right. Anyway, I've made reservations at a motel near I-70 and Noland Road and printed MapQuest directions from there to your house and to Dennis and Richie's. It looks like a good location for me."

He gave her his cell phone number and hung up.

Imagine that, Molly thought, *a man who isn't afraid to ask for directions and offers to help before he's asked. Of course, that probably means he's an anal-retentive, nit-picking control freak. Great. This ought to be loads of fun.*

She tried to remember what she'd heard about Dennis's parents. It wasn't much. She knew his mother had died a few years ago. His dad still lived in Colorado Springs, where Dennis grew up, and she thought he was retired, but she wasn't sure from what.

Richie and Dennis went to visit Gil a couple of times a year and when Dennis talked about his dad, his tone was affectionate. He seldom mentioned his mom.

~~

When Molly called to make the arrangements for Gil's visit, Richie put her on the speakerphone so she could talk to him and Dennis at the same time. She hated the speakerphone. It sounded like they were talking into a barrel and she couldn't tell if they were speaking to her or to each other.

"I think Friday night's okay, isn't it,"
Richie said. There was a long silence.

Molly finally said, "I already told you it's alright with me."

16

"I know, Mom. I was talking to Dennis. He's thinking."

"Well, when you two get through thinking, one of you can call me back. And don't put me on the damn speaker again."

Richie called back 10 minutes later. "Okay, Mom, here's the plan. No restaurant. Since we'll be discussing our unholy union, it's probably best if we don't do it in public. Dennis and I will bring steaks and all the trimmings to your house and we'll take care of the preparations. Can you handle dessert?"

"It's the least I can do." She allowed sarcasm to drip into the phone. "I'll bake some brownies."

"Oh, Mom, brownies are so pedestrian."

"Fine, I'll surprise you."

"Oh, dear God," Richie groaned.

~~

Molly picked up a gorgeous raspberry torte from *The Pastry Goddess* on Friday morning. Then she went home and baked brownies. She taste- tested one, sealed the rest in a Tupperware container and stowed them in a cupboard with the canned goods.

Richie and Dennis descended midafternoon and occupied her kitchen like a couple of prissy warriors on a culinary mission. They unloaded steaks, spices, baking potatoes, salad fixings and two bottles of wine. They assembled and inspected their weapons —Molly's barbecue tools. Richie took a couple of white aprons from one of their sacks and they each put one on. Both aprons had *Master Chef* printed across the bib.

Molly retreated to a stool on the far side of the counter and watched them fuss over every detail. She had observed them at a couple of their remodel sites, supervising a crew of construction workers, and she was amused at their ability to change personas to fit the situation. When they stepped into their steel-toed boots, donned their hard hats and strapped on their tool belts, they shed their effeminate mannerisms, spoke with lower voices and occasionally spit on the ground.

However, Molly knew what she was watching at the moment was the real deal. Dennis concocted a mysterious marinade for the steaks, a secret recipe he claimed to have learned from his dad. When Molly wanted to know what he was putting in it, Dennis acted as if he'd been asked to give up state secrets.

Richie scrubbed four perfect baking potatoes and wrapped them in foil. He began to put together a salad that made Molly blush in shame for the pre-chopped and bagged varieties she usually settled on. Dennis reached over Richie's shoulder to pluck a cherry tomato out of the bowl and got his hand slapped.

I could get used to this, Molly thought — *food preparation, entertainment — and no cover charge.*

The doorbell rang at precisely 6:30. Molly opened the door to a tall silver-haired man, with a bouquet of flowers in his hand.

"Are those for me," she asked, "or do you have the wrong house?"

"If you're Molly, they're for you."

"And if you're Gil, it's the right house. Come on in before the flowers wilt."

He stepped inside and gave her a once-over. "I can see where Richie gets his good looks."

"And I can see where Dennis gets his good taste." Gil handed her the bouquet.

"Thanks. The last man who brought me flowers stayed 20 years, but don't let that scare you," she said as she gave them a sniff.

"Come on out to the kitchen. I wouldn't want you to miss another minute of the show those two are putting on."

"I've seen them cook before," Gil said. "Is it time to take away the sharp instruments?"

Molly didn't have a dining room as such. It was more of an extension of the kitchen. That was where they found Richie, putting the finishing touches on the table. Dennis was coming through the door from the deck where he'd been checking on the gas grill. They both dropped everything to greet Gil.

There was an exuberant exchange of hugs, handshakes, fist bumps, little punches on the shoulder. Watching, Molly thought how the male greeting ritual transcended sexual orientation. She laid the flowers on the counter, picked up her Waterford crystal vase (received in lieu of male stripper) from the center of the table and went to the sink to fill it with water. She turned around in time to see Dennis step back from his dad and give him a head-to-toe appraisal.

Gil wore a light green polo tucked into khaki-colored chinos. Brown leather moccasins and a matching belt completed the ensemble.

"Looking pretty good for a geezer, Dad. You've put yourself together rather nicely."

"Why thanks, son. 'Queer Eye for the Straight Guy' changed my life."

Molly felt a surge of admiration for this man, for the easy, graceful way he accepted the role of being the father of a gay son.

During dinner, Richie and Dennis regaled Gil with every detail of their trip to California to "do the real deed" as Richie put it.

"Has anyone been critical of your plans for this wedding?" Gil asked.

"One so-called friend, make that former friend, suggested it was a sham," Dennis said. "I told him to kiss my tender sweet ass and removed his name from the guest list."

~~

The steaks were perfect. Gil praised the food and the chefs.

Molly repeated one of her favorite phrases, "It's easy to love a guy who cooks."

While they waited for the main course to settle before tackling dessert, Richie and Dennis cleared the table and brewed a pot of coffee. Dennis filled coffee cups and Richie brought Molly's torte to the table. He had removed it from the Pastry Goddess box and presented it on a pink pedestal cake plate, part of a collection of Depression glass that usually gathered dust in Molly's china cabinet.

Gil eyed the fancy confection without enthusiasm. "I'm not sure I can eat another bite," he said.

Molly watched them sip coffee and ignore the torte for a few minutes, before she excused herself. She got the brownies from the cupboard, removed the lid and set the Tupperware container in the middle of the table. Then she brought a tub of vanilla ice cream and a scoop with her and sat down again. "Dessert, anyone?"

Richie covered his face with his hands.

Gil said, "Now that's more like it. Don't mind if I do." He grabbed two brownies from the container and set it down to help himself to ice cream without passing either around the table.

Dennis said, "Ooh, Mollymoms, you made brownies," and reached for one.

In the end, Richie succumbed to a brownie alamode along with the rest of them. Molly caught his eye and smiled sweetly. She considered it her motherly duty to poke a hole in his pretentiousness from time to time.

Chapter 5

"Come to find out, Dennis's dad and I didn't need to worry." Molly lounged on the deck with a cup of coffee and the cordless phone, while she related the previous night's events to Liz. "Richie and Dennis have every- thing planned, right down to a gnat's ass."

"Wow," Liz said. "That's so...gay. They were probably afraid you two wouldn't have a clue."

"And they'd be right. I mean, how do you plan a wedding with two grooms? What is that supposed to look like?"

"I don't know," Liz said, "but I wouldn't miss one outlandish minute of it."

"You'd stop and gawk at a bloody wreck on the highway." "So what's his dad like?" Liz asked.

"Nothing like I expected. I pictured him as a kind of Wilford Brimley when I talked to him on the phone. I thought he had a fat voice — you know sort of deep and resonant. But he's more of a Dick Van Dyke. He's tall like Dennis, but not skinny."

"So he's fat?"

"No, not fat at all. Average. Starting to get just a little thick around the middle. Trim mustache, full head of hair. His hair and mustache are totally white, but I'll bet he used to be blonde, like Dennis, because he has that kind of golden tan that only blondes get. And the tan really sets off his white hair and blue eyes."

"So he's hot, then?"

"I didn't think of him as hot. I guess you'd call him handsome. Natty dresser — does casual with more style than most men — or women for that matter. Dennis even complimented him on his choice of clothing."

"No kidding?"

"And get this. He used MapQuest directions to find my house, arrived at precisely the appointed time and brought flowers. He seems very proper but he also has a surprising sense of humor."

"Wait," Liz said. "Is gayness hereditary?"

"I have to admit it crossed my mind. But I know it's not the case with Richie. His dad had his faults but he passed the test in that department."

"I guess you're right. And since you've never tried to put the move on me, I have to assume you're straight — or else you don't find me attractive."

"The truth's out," Molly said, "you're just not my type. I've got another call. Talk to you later." She flashed to the incoming call.

"Mom, are you busy?"

"Never too busy for my favorite daughter." She cradled the phone between her shoulder and ear and carried her coffee inside.

"Thanks, Mom. That really means a lot from the perspective of an only daughter."

"True, but I'm sure you'd still be my favorite, even if there were others. What's up?"

"I saw they printed another one of your grammar rants on the Opinions Page the other day."

"Yeah, my claim to fame."

Molly had written to complain about the semi-literate meteorologist on a local TV channel and his continual assault on the English language. The two examples she cited were: "We see it cooling off in the fairly recent future," and "It's almost next to impossible to predict."

"Mom, the thing is Gus saw it. He reads the Opinions Page every morning before he goes to school. Most kids read the funnies if they even look at the paper. But not my Gus. He reads the Opinions Page."

"So what's wrong with that? If he disagrees with my opinion, he should write his own letter. I'd be proud of him for taking a stand."

"Oh, he doesn't disagree with you, and you know it. Every time he sees one of your letters, he takes the paper to school and shows it off. He especially liked the last one.

"Mom, are you aware that he collects assignment notes and memos from his teacher and corrects her grammar and punctuation?"

"Okay, Sophie, I'm waiting for you to tell me why that's a bad thing." "It's a bad thing because it gets him in trouble. After he showed off your last letter, a bunch of the kids got up a collection of red pencils for him to give his grandma. So Gus-of-the-quick-comeback says, "Thanks, guys, but I think I'll keep them to correct all of Mrs. Carter's mistakes. Maybe it'll be enough to last through the school year.""

"Unfortunately, Mrs. Carter overheard the conversation and asked him to explain himself, which prompted Gus to bring her a stack of her notes, complete with his corrections, yesterday morning."

"Oh, no. What did she do?"

"Gus said she sifted through them, then looked at him over her glasses, and stuck them in her desk drawer."

"What do you suppose she's going to do with them?"

"We'll never know. Gus told her they were his property and demanded she give them back. She did, reluctantly, but you can imagine he must be right at the top of her shit list now. I'm just waiting for a call from her."

Molly's heart filled with love and pride at the image of her tall, skinny, bespectacled 12-year-old grandson taking a righteous stand in the interest of good grammar.

"Admit it, Sophie. Aren't you just a little proud of him?"

"Sure," Sophie sighed. "How could I not be? The kid's a near genius. I just get a little worried about him being so — you know — studious. I hope I didn't waste a great name like Gus."

"Oh, for God's sake, Sophie. Get over it. You've never caught him playing with dolls or getting into your makeup, have you? Besides, do you think it would have made a difference if I had named your brother Duke?"

"He'd probably have changed it to Duchess."

"Sophie—"

"Just kidding, Mom. You know I love Richie just the way he is."

After they hung up, it occurred to Molly that Sophie hadn't expressed an iota of concern about Mrs. Carter's incompetence. She resisted the urge to call her back.

Chapter 6

It felt like jumping off a cliff when Molly finally agreed to go on the cruise. The reservations had been made and now she was shopping, with Jan's close supervision, for the proper clothing.

Jan pulled a pantsuit from the rack and held it up for Molly's consideration.

"It's too busy." Molly dismissed it with barely a glance.

"What do you mean, busy?"

"Well, just look at it. The pants have little stripes and the top has geometric patterns."

"So? They're color coordinated and it all works together nicely."

"Not for me, it doesn't."

Jan put it back, rummaged through the rack some more, and pulled out another selection. This one was a soft, dressy pantsuit with the pants in a variegated blue/green pattern and a solid light green top. "How about this?"

"Nope." Molly shook her head.

"What's wrong with it?"

"Why do the pants have to be different from the top? Why can't it all be one color?"

"For heaven's sake, Molly. Do you have to be so monochromatic?"

"I know what that means, Jan. And I happen to like monochromatic. It's slimming. If I put different colors and patterns on the top and bottom, I look like two mismatched parts welded together by mistake."

"Couldn't you at least try it?"

"It'd be a waste of time. I know I wouldn't like it."

Jan shoved the pantsuit back in its slot and turned to Molly with her hands on her hips. "Then pick something you do like.

And could you step up the pace a little? The ship sails in two weeks."

Molly giggled. "Jan, you're actually tapping your foot. You look like a disgruntled schoolteacher."

"Good grief, Molly. Can you be serious for once?"

"Okay, okay. It's just that I don't know where to start. I don't know what to wear and I don't know how to act." She shoved her hands deep into the pockets of her jeans and stared at the floor.

"That's what I'm here for," Jan said. "I'll help you find something to wear. Just work with me, okay?"

"Fine, I'll let you pick something for me. But don't try to get me into khaki shorts with a blue shirt," she said, eyeing a nearby mannequin with distaste. "That's just wrong."

Unleashed by Molly's agreement to work with her, Jan moved through the racks of clothing with a single-minded ferocity. She grabbed one garment after another, rejecting this one, selecting that one, until her arms were loaded. "Okay, let's go try them on."

Molly followed her toward the dressing rooms. "Isn't there a limit to how many things you can bring in at one time?"

"If you stick your nose in the air and act like you own the place, nobody will say a word."

For the next hour, Molly tried on at least two dozen outfits under Jan's watchful eye. As she struggled out of a long, silky shift, Molly whined, "Are you sure I need something like this?"

"Yes. That'll be great for dinner. It's just dressy enough without being over the top. And it'll also be perfect for outings like the theater when we get back."

"Which means what I wore to the theater was *not* right. *I knew it.* As soon as I saw you and Margot, I knew it. I felt like a pair of scuffed up penny loafers hanging out with Cinderella's slippers."

"Well, I won't let that happen again, I promise. That's why we're here."

"Jan, is it too late to back out? I'm really feeling panicky about this trip. I'm getting stressed because it's too close to the wedding. And I'm not thrilled about being dressed up properly and trotted out in front of your snooty friends for more evenings at the the-ay'-tah."

"Molly, what's wrong with you? Ever since you decided to retire early, you've been talking about how you couldn't wait to expand your horizons—get acquainted with new people, go places you've never been and do new things. You're such an enigma!"

"Careful, Jan. I know what that means."

"Of course you know what it means. You work crossword puzzles in ink. You know what everything means. You're one the smartest people I know to be such a dumbass sometimes. And that's just one example of what makes you an enigma. You're smart enough to know what it means, but you're so insecure you think I don't know you know. Now you've got me talking in circles. What's really bothering you?"

"Well, for one thing, I'm not sure I want to be a part of a foursome that includes three women and one man. I miss Sam and I miss being half of a couple. And, no offence, but I wanted to see the world with Sam."

"Well now, that's not an option any more, is it? Besides, when Sam was alive, you used to complain that he never wanted to do anything cultural. And if he were alive, would he have gone with you to see Phantom of the Opera?"

"Probably not. I think the word opera would have put him off. But if he had gone with me, he wouldn't have gotten all worked up about whom was more," she made finger quotes, "*convincing* in the *production*."

Jan ignored the sarcasm and said, "Well, now you have a chance to be friends with people who will do things like that with you and you're still not happy. It seems to me like you want to go to the symphony or ballet and you want to be escorted by a cowboy with barnyard stuff clinging to his boots." She snickered.

"I don't know where you came up with that. I never said anything about a cowboy. And for your information, that barnyard stuff is called horseshit."

Jan pushed aside a pile of garments and sat down on the dressing room bench. "Why do you always do this, Molly?"

"Do what?"

27

"Resort to crude language and go for the shock effect when you don't want to face an issue."

"What? You're shocked by horseshit?" Molly tossed the silky shift at Jan and grabbed her jeans. "I'm through. I'll take the damn slinky shift. I'll take everything that fits. Let's just get out of here."

"Come on, Molly. Talk to me. If you don't want to hang out with me and my friends, what *do* you want?"

"I don't know. Maybe a good old boy who'll dress up and take me to the ballet, then take me out for pizza and a beer afterward— to someplace where they throw peanut shells on the floor."

And I'd like him to have a truck, she thought.

Molly's mood improved in the shoe department where an eager to please young man patiently brought her one pair of shoes after another. It was infinitely easier to sit there and relax and be waited on than it had been to struggle in and out of piles of clothing.

However, her mood took another downward spiral when she got home and added up the receipts from her purchases. No matter that she had set aside money for the purpose and could afford it. She had never spent that much on herself at one time in her life. She couldn't help feeling as if she'd taken the food right out of —well— *someone's* mouth.

Chapter 7

Jan closed her umbrella and stepped through Molly's door. "Just one more week! My God, I can't wait to set sail and leave this godforsaken Midwest weather behind. It's not supposed to be this cold at this time of year."

Molly took Jan's raincoat and hung it on the coat rack. "You're right," she said. "It's cold as a well digger's ass. What could be important enough to get you out on a night like this?"

"I was out at Independence Center. I hope you don't mind my dropping by." She followed Molly into the kitchen. "Oops, I didn't realize you had company."

I'm surprised the extra car in the driveway didn't tip you off, Molly thought but resisted saying.

Richie said, "Hi, Aunt Jan. You've met Dennis, haven't you?"

Jan was obviously more interested in the simmering crock-pot on the counter than she was in Richie's friend. "I believe we've met. Hi, Dennis. Molly, is that beef stew? Mmmm. It smells wonderful. And what a perfect day for it."

Molly did a mental eye roll and the guys studiously avoided looking at each other. Jan's radar for dropping in at mealtime was legendary.

"Jan, you may as well join us. I was just getting ready to take the biscuits out of the oven."

"Are you sure there's enough?"

"Of course, there's enough. I've never mastered the art of cooking for less than an army." She slid the biscuits from the baking sheet into a cloth-lined basket and set them on the table.

"Wow, thanks." Jan settled herself at the far side of the table and then asked, "Is there anything I can do to help."

"Not a thing." *Now that you're all comfy*, Molly thought, then immediately chided herself. *Surely I don't begrudge her a bowl of stew and a biscuit.*

She quickly set an extra place at the table. Then she lifted the stoneware bowl out of the crockpot and placed it on a copper trivet in the center of the table. She stuck a ladle in the bowl and said, "It's casual dining tonight. Richie, will you open the wine, please. I'll get the glasses."

Dennis began serving the stew while Molly brought the glasses to the table and Richie brought the wine. He politely started to pour Jan's wine first.

"Wait!" She held her hand over the glass. "Molly, may I ask you a question?" she said and promptly asked it without waiting for Molly's response. "Why are you using champagne flutes for wine? Don't you have wine glasses?"

Dennis paused with a ladle full of stew and Richie stood with the bottle of wine suspended over Jan's glass.

Molly picked up one of the long-stemmed, slender glasses and looked at it. It was a champagne flute? She knew exactly why she used these glasses for wine. They held five ounces. She could have four ounces of wine for three Weight Watcher points and she figured the extra ounce wouldn't hurt.

So she knew the reason why she used these and left the fatter ones (the real wine glasses, according to Jan) in the cupboard, but she hadn't known the difference. And what the hell did it matter, anyway? She doubted that Jan meant to be helpful. She just couldn't pass up an opportunity to point out Molly's lack of sophistication.

Molly grabbed the flutes from in front of Jan, Richie and Dennis, returned them to the cupboard and replaced them with real wine glasses. Without a word, Richie poured wine into the three wine glasses and filled the flute Molly stubbornly left in front of her own plate.

They sat and began to eat. It was a silent meal.

Molly had no sooner started to clear the table than Jan became concerned about the weather and announced she had better scoot before she had to deal with flooded streets.

Chapter 8

Molly called Jan early the next morning. "I can't go on the cruise."

"What's wrong? Why can't you go?"

"Because I don't know a fucking champagne flute from a fucking wine glass!" Molly slammed the phone down.

She went back to bed and tried to ignore the persistent ringing of the phone and Jan's strident voice on her answering machine. After a half hour, she got up and went from room to room, unplugging all the phones in the house. She turned off her cell phone, crawled back into bed and lay there until she drifted off to sleep.

She was awakened by the sound of the doorbell. She opened one eye and looked at the clock. It was after 11 a.m., and she still didn't want to see or talk to anyone. Well, she would just ignore it.

She heard the front door open. "Mollymoms?" Footsteps went from room to room before they finally came down the hall. There was a knock on her bedroom door.

"Mollymoms, open the door!"

Jan and everyone else had given up and left her alone a couple of hours ago. Now here was her gay-as-pink-ink-whatever-in-law demanding to be let in.

"Come on, Mollymoms, sweetheart. Open up. I've got chocolate and booze. And I've come to help you diss the sugly ister-in-law. Now let me in before I'm forced to use my brute strength and knock down the door."

The silly spoonerism did it and the smile Molly tried to suppress finally won.

She got off the bed, pulled on her robe and unlocked the door.

Dennis darted in, a margarita in one hand and a box of chocolates in the other. "It's afternoon somewhere." He set the margarita on the nightstand, shoved the chocolates into her hand and ordered her to "eat, drink, vent."

Molly propped herself against the pillows and reached for the margarita. She tried to look angry with this beautiful young man, immaculate and stylish from his spiked blonde hair to his highly polished black boots. He wore a long sleeved white cotton shirt, tucked into black jeans that rode low on his slender hips. She had a disturbing insight that he might turn out to be her favorite child, DNA notwithstanding.

"Okay, Dennis, who sent you? And how did you get in my house?" "I'm doing an intervention, darling. Jan's been calling everyone in the family and they've been calling each other. Then Richie came whining to me." He put his hands on his hips and rolled his eyes. "I suppose it's a test to see how I fit into this nutty family.

"As to how I got in, let me just say this: If you ever decide to have a steamy affair, you'll need to change your locks and resist the urge to hand out keys to your children and friends. Now, let's see what Jan talked you into buying for a trip you don't want to take. Dear God, doesn't she put you in mind of a yapping Chihuahua?"

He marched to Molly's closet and flung open the door as if he owned the place. "I want to see everything that still has a price tag on it."

"That's easy," Molly said, "it's all still in the garment bags." She took a healthy slug of the margarita and sighed.

Dennis piled the newly purchased clothing on the king-size bed and slid the bags from over the hangers. "Scoot, scoot, scoot," he flicked his hand at Molly. "I need room to work here."

Molly took the chocolates and the margarita and moved to the rocker.

Dennis began to separate the items into groups that seemed to make sense only to him. He held each garment up by the hanger, cast an appraising eye from it, to Molly, and back again, before each pronouncement: "It's not you.

"So not you.

"Hmmm, I'll come back to this.

"This would make you look like an overstuffed Jan.

"This has possibilities.

"What in God's name could the woman have been thinking?"

Each item was rated, or berated, then assigned to the appropriate pile, according to Dennis.

"Now for the footwear, Mollymoms. Let's see the shoes."

Good Lord, I'm getting fashion advice from a flaming fairy, she thought, but she meekly gestured toward four shoeboxes stacked in the corner.

Dennis appraised the shoes, pronounced one pair keepers and tossed the other three boxes onto the return pile. He grabbed a note pad and pen from the nightstand and totaled the price tags on the returns.

"Now let's see what we can do about the airline ticket. I just happen to have a friend in high places." He wiggled his eyebrows. "Maybe that and the clothing refund will make your non-refundable cruise ticket a little less painful." He whipped out his tiny cell phone and punched in numbers.

Molly drained her margarita and set the glass down. She felt a rush of euphoria. It could have been the margarita on an empty stomach, but it could just as well have been the fact that someone had finally given her permission to chuck the stupid cruise.

"Oh, and one more thing, Mollymoms," Dennis said on his way out. "I left an interesting article on the kitchen table. Don't feel picked on. I sent the same one to my dad. Read it." And he was gone, with an air kiss and a dainty finger wave.

It was an article about Internet dating for seniors.

Chapter 9

Molly entered the Senior Matchmaker website surreptitiously. She took a deep breath and told herself to forge ahead. She had too many hours invested in the process to quit now.

She spent two of those hours trying to set up a second email account and a separate identity on her own, then another two hours on the phone with various tech support people. These were the same people, she suspected, who wrote instruction manuals for cell phones. Her end of the dialogue went mostly like this: "Excuse me, I'm sorry, could you repeat that? You want me to purr down — what now? Oh, *pull* down — what? And crick? No? Click! Click where?"

But it was finally done. She had chosen a password consisting of random numbers and letters, and a handle (dreamcatcher). She was ready to set up her profile.

You want to meet: The checklist included *Man, Woman, Couples (man and woman), Group (two or more people).* Holy shit! She clicked *Man*, and moved on.

Introduction Title: With her marketing background, Molly would have described this as a tag line. She typed in, *"Regular gal looking for a regular guy.* That seemed safe enough.

Next. *Introduction Text (e.g. describe who you are and what you like/dislike.* There was a link that led to *Suggestions/Help.* It was full of lines like "most of my friends would say I have a (fill in blank) personality" and "one of the more interesting things I've done in my life is (finish sentence)." She decided she could handle this without their suggestions. She wrote: I'm funny, sincere, smart, and sometimes outspoken. I enjoy reading. I work crossword puzzles in ink. I listen to a variety of music, from classical to country (no hard rock or rap). I like to walk nature trails in the area, and I love to dance.

Moving On. *Describe what you're looking for in a person.* Another link to *Suggestions/Help.* "I like going out on dates, meeting new people," and "I know there's chemistry between my date and I if (blank)." Her internal grammar Nazi reared its head and screeched, "...between my date and **me**. Doesn't anyone edit this stuff?"

Again she declined and went with her own text: "I'm looking for someone who is interested in friendship, dating and possibly developing a relationship. Someone who can be with me but also has interests of his own. If you're clingy, possessive or controlling, save us both some time and don't contact me." Molly paused. She wondered if that was a little too blunt, but she gave a mental shrug and continued: "I'm pretty independent but I miss everything that goes with being part of a couple. There's a lot more to know about me, but I'll leave something to talk about over coffee."

The next area was *Physical Information. Age:* 63 *Height:* 5' 4" *Body Type:* This was a pull-down list. The choices were: *Prefer not to say, Average, Slim/petite, Athletic, Ample, A little extra padding, Large.*

She mentally deducted the 10 pounds she still intended to lose and chose *Average* instead of *Extra Padding.*

Holy crap, Molly snarled at the computer as her eye traveled down the long list of questions. I'm trying to meet a man, not apply for a position with Homeland Security. And she began skipping questions and combining answers.

Hair Color: She typed: *Only my hairdresser remembers but what you'll see is brown, short, and naturally curly.*

Blue eyes, sometimes glasses, sometimes contacts.

She finished with: *Live in Independence, Missouri, non-smoker, social drinker, widow.* She skipped Religion (she wasn't sure herself) and Education. Smart enough not to say "between my date and I" she groused, but left it blank.

She narrowed the search criteria to *man, within a 50-mile radius, between 60 and 70 years old,* and hit the browse button. Some listings had a photo, some didn't. Each one had a handle, a tag line, his age and where he lived. The person's handle was a link that opened a page with all the other information.

Molly scrolled through several entries, glancing at the handles and tag lines. It didn't take long to confirm what she feared. If there were any normal men on this website, they were outnumbered by the lunatic fringe.

Some of the handles could only be described as perverted — like hot-tongue4u. Do men really think women like that kind of stuff? Are there women who do? Then there was hotpassion67 (she wondered what was in his prescription bottle) and sniffer69 (she didn't even want to think about that one).

Some of the handles and tag lines were innocuous, but stupid. For example: daytimelover; tag line, "When the sun shines Im ready are you". *Has he ever heard of punctuation?*

And how about this one? Handle, lovingman4u: tag line, "You had me at hello." How original. Does he think he's the only one who's seen that movie?

She clicked on silverfox72, no photo, tagline, "I'm looking for that special lady." The bio opened to reveal what silverfox 72 was looking for in a woman: "72-year-old man seeks slender, attractive woman, nice legs, age 30-45, to share good times."

Molly shook her head at the audacity. "And just what," she sneered at the screen, "makes you think such a prize would be interested in your wrinkled old ass!"

She closed the site, turned off her computer and went to wash her hands.

~~

"Oh, come on, Molly. You've paid for a month. You might as well give it a chance." Liz opened the refrigerator and helped herself to a Diet Pepsi.

"Haven't you been listening, Liz? The site is full of perverts and illiterates with inflated opinions of themselves. One of them, a guy from California, sent me a message that said, 'Where's your picture? You wouldn't go fishing without bait, would you?' Bait! Bait is a worm or a crawdad or raw liver. And I'm not about to put my picture out there for these creeps to look at. I can't help thinking about what some of them might do while they're looking at my picture."

Liz jumped up and grabbed Molly's hand. "Show me the site!"

Molly hung back. "Why? Am I about to find out my best friend is a closet pervert?"

"Whatcha mean, closet? Now come on. Show me. I'll help you find someone."

Molly sighed, picked up her coffee and followed Liz into the office. She might as well. There was no stopping Liz when she was on a roll. And she was on a definite roll.

Liz pulled a chair up next to Molly's and waited while she logged on and began to browse through the listings. "Hot damn, it's like a stud muffin catalog." She scooted closer, forcing Molly to move over.

"Liz, you've got the last good man on earth and here you are getting all lathered up over a bunch of men on a website."

"I'm getting lathered up on your behalf. Just trying to help a friend."

"Yeah, right."

Molly had been scrolling through the pages at a fairly fast pace when one of the pictures caught her eye. She backed up. "Look, Liz. Doesn't he remind you of Sam?"

"I was ready to say that's wishful thinking on your part, but darned if he doesn't. A little."

Molly clicked on the link and they both leaned in to read the bio. His handle was "beau jest" and the tagline was "Friends first."

"Beau jest?" Molly said. "He's either got a clever sense of humor or he's sending a warning."

"Maybe he's not a movie buff," Liz said.

"Nor much of a bookworm," Molly said. "Let's investigate."

His bio said he weighed 235 pounds, but he was 6' 4". If he looked like Sam, he would certainly be a larger version. They printed his photo and studied it. He might be a little barrel-chested, but at 6' 4", he wouldn't be fat, just big. They scoured the rest of his profile looking for anything suspicious.

"He seems normal," Liz pronounced. "Let's make contact!" Molly composed a message:

"Hi, I'm dreamcatcher. I've just read your profile and it seems like we have a lot in common. I'd be interested in hearing from you." She attached her profile and hit *SEND*.

Beau responded that evening without asking for a photo of her—a point in his favor. Over the next three days they exchanged several messages and finally agreed to meet for lunch. Beau suggested a Best Burgers north of the river. Molly responded that if he was partial to Best Burgers, there was one on 40 Highway, nearer to her home and she would rather meet there than try to find one she wasn't familiar with. Beau assured her he would have no trouble at all finding the one near her, and it was a date. She told him she'd be driving a grey Mercury and that she'd meet him in the parking lot at 1 o'clock on Friday. In his last message, he said his name was Bob. She responded, "I'm Molly. I'll see you on Friday."

Chapter 10

Liz followed Molly to the Gordman's parking lot across the highway from Best Burgers. The plan was for Liz to wait for 15 minutes, drive across the highway, come in, and get a table as close as possible to Molly and her date.

Molly pulled into Best Burgers at 12:59. She made a slow circuit around the west side of the lot looking for the white Suburban Bob had described. She didn't see it. Maybe she was a little early. She parked where she could see the entrance to the parking lot and checked her watch. It was 1 o'clock on the dot. Maybe he ran into heavy traffic. She would wait five minutes, not a minute longer. She pulled down the visor and opened the mirror for one last nervous inspection of her makeup. In the reflection she saw a man come out of the restaurant, pause a moment, then walk toward her car. That couldn't be him. He didn't look tall enough. She flipped the visor up and turned to face him as he approached her car door.

He looked through the window and mouthed the question, "Molly?"

She nodded and opened the door.

"Hi, I'm Bob. I thought that was you. I'm parked on the other side of the building so I figured you hadn't seen my Suburban." He continued talking as Molly pulled her keys out of the ignition, picked up her handbag and got out of the car.

He reached for her hand as she stood to face him. "It's nice to meet you, Molly."

Molly was stunned. If he was 6' 4" her eyes should have been on a level with his middle shirt button instead of his eyes. His face bore some resemblance to his photo on the website and he had obviously been truthful about his weight, if not his height. And to think she had worried about fudging her weight by 10 pounds!

Molly hadn't said a word yet, but Bob didn't seem to notice. He was still talking. He took off the Mizzou cap he wore and waved it under her nose. "As you can see, I'm a Tigers' fan. I graduated from MU in '62. I played defense the last two years. We won almost all of our games those two years."

He stuck the cap back on his head, took Molly's arm and headed for the restaurant. Besides the Mizzou cap, he wore a red windbreaker over a plaid shirt, faded blue jeans and a pair of Reeboks that had seen whiter days.

By the time they reached the door, Molly had learned he was divorced, retired from the Marines and drove a school bus part of the year.

He held the door open for her and led the way to a table with the remnants of a meal on it. "I got here early so I went ahead and ate lunch. But you just order whatever you want. They have great shakes here."

A waiter appeared and began clearing the mess on Bob's side of the table. Bob said, "You can bring me a cup of coffee and see what the little lady here would like."

"I'll have a cup of coffee while I think about it," Molly said. She was sure it was the first time Bob had heard her voice.

Before the waiter could leave to get her coffee, Bob said to him, "Say son, didn't you used to work at the Best Burgers up north?"

"Sure did. I thought you looked familiar."

"Yeah, I usually frequent that one. How long ago did you work there?" He went on without waiting for an answer. "You probably knew David, can't remember his last name, a skinny red-haired guy, talked with a stutter. You may remember me from the time I brought a whole busload of kids in after their basketball game. They were sure wound up because they'd won, but I managed to keep them corralled."

Bob kept talking at the waiter for another five minutes, while Molly waited for her coffee and watched Liz come in and get seated at the nearest empty table several feet away.

The waiter finally escaped and Bob turned back to Molly. "Well, now, let me tell you a little about myself." For the next half hour, Molly sipped coffee and listened to Bob expound on his military career, how he'd excelled in football, how much he loved driving a school bus—it wasn't for the money, of course. He didn't need the money, but he enjoyed the young people. He was strict but fair and felt sure he had earned both their affection and respect.

When he finally stopped to take a sip of cold coffee, Molly jumped in. "Well. Enough about you, Bob." She smiled as she said it to take the edge off the sarcasm. "Let me tell you a little about myself. I'm a widow. My husband died two years ago. I retired last month. I'd been with the same company for over 20 years."

She paused slightly, giving him a chance to ask what kind of work she had done, but he didn't, so she went on. "Let's see. I read a lot, I like to work crossword puzzles and I'm pretty good at it if I do say so."

Bob's eyes were fixed on her, but there wasn't a flicker of emotion or interest in his gaze. It was as if he were looking at the far side of somewhere else. Molly found it disconcerting, but she forged ahead.

"Uhm, I've been thinking about taking piano lessons now that I have more free time. That's something I've always wanted to do. Or get involved in some kind of volunteer work or maybe politics or..."

"Politics!" Bob came to life with a jolt. "Now, if you want to get involved in politics, I could introduce you to some of our state officials. I do a lot of volunteer political work — go to a lot of meetings, know everyone. In fact, I'm pretty much a fixture at the Republican headquarters in St. Joseph. Would you like me to—"

"Wait, wait, wait," Molly held up both hands. "I'm afraid you're knocking on the wrong door, Bob. I'm a bleeding-heart, tree-hugging, liberal Democrat."

Bob leaned back in his chair and crossed his arms over his chest. "Really? You seem like a fairly intelligent woman, Molly. I would have thought you'd be a Republican."

Molly grabbed her handbag and stood up so fast her chair toppled over. "I don't have any reason to suspect you're intelligent, Bob. But I did think you'd be taller." She turned and stomped out of the restaurant.

She was so angry she was still shaking by the time Liz screeched to a halt beside her at the far end of the Gordman's parking lot, jerked open the passenger door and slid in. "What happened?"

"Oh, my God." Molly dug in her handbag and came out with a wad of Kleenex. Her carefully applied makeup was dissolving in a wash of tears. "What an insufferable, bloated egomaniac! I should have left as soon as I found out he'd already eaten. Liz, what kind of a jerk makes a date to meet a woman for lunch and eats before she gets there?"

"He ate before you got there?"

"Yes, and I still kept wanting to find something good about him. I was so hung up on thinking he looked like Sam. But you know what? The more he talked, the less he reminded me of Sam and now I feel like I dishonored Sam's memory by ever even thinking he did."

"Okay, here's what we're going to do," Liz said. "Lock up your car and get in with me. I'm taking you to lunch. I'll pop for something classier than burgers and fries. And you'll tell me all about it. Every word."

Liz drove to V's, where they ate pasta and shared a bottle of wine while Molly recounted every pathetic detail of her first date in 20 years. Ending with a tearful, "Oh, Liz, there aren't any good men left. I'm afraid I'm never going to have sex again."

Liz reached across the table and patted Molly's hand. "Honey, if sex is all you want, you can find it at the Republican headquarters in St. Joseph."

"You're right." Molly stared into her wine glass. "I may talk Erica Jong but I've got straight lace sticking out all over me."

Chapter 11

On May 30, Molly pulled into the parking lot of the Jones Funeral Home in Odessa. She turned off her windshield wipers and reached for her umbrella. *Was this damned rain ever going to stop,* she wondered as she had a fleeting image of Jan sunning herself on a ship's deck somewhere in the middle of the Caribbean. She flipped the umbrella open and tried to avoid stepping in a puddle as she made her way from the car to the building.

This was the third funeral she had attended in six days and her right big toe screamed in protest at the constriction of the black pumps she had grown unaccustomed to since the end of April. First it was a former coworker who had died after a long battle with cancer. Next was a neighbor— a widow who lived two doors down the street. And now it was Molly's oldest cousin, Paul, who had dropped dead halfway between his house and his street-side mailbox.

The actual funeral service would follow an hour long visitation, which was in progress. Molly had barely finished signing the guest book when she was cornered by a younger cousin, Debbie, whom she hadn't seen in several years.

Debbie doggedly pointed out which of the grown men and women were her children and which of the youngsters were her grandchildren. "Oh, and you haven't met my daughter-in-law, Gretchen. Wait right here. I'll grab her and bring her over."

As she turned to search for an escape route, Molly's attention was drawn to a tall, gangly man who stepped inside the foyer and stood looking around as if he were lost. When he saw Molly, he slapped his forehead, pointed at her and threw his hand over his heart in a dramatic flourish. He started toward her, holding out both arms.

Who in God's name...? He wore a shiny brown suit, a blue and white striped shirt, and a pair of scuffed cowboy boots. Recognition came slowly. The shock of unruly white hair that used to be red, the twinkling blue eyes that now had laugh crinkles at the corners, and the same wide smile.

"Molly Ladd!" He grabbed her hands and stepped back as if to admire her. "Ohmygosh! You're still beautiful. You haven't changed a bit."

"And neither have you, Charley Hickman. You're still full of it. And it's Stark now."

"Huh?"

"Stark, not Ladd."

"Oh, well, ohmygosh. Anyhoo, I guess you're surprised to see me here. I saw the obit in the paper and I knew it was Paul by the list of survivors."

"Yeah, pretty surprised. We all lost track of you after you and Ginger were divorced. Did you remarry?"

"Twice more, after your lovely cousin, Ginger. But anyhoo, neither one of them worked out either. What about you? Is there a Mr. uhm Stark, was it, with you?"

"No, I lost him two years ago." *My god,* Molly thought. *That sounds like I misplaced him.* "I mean he died two years ago," she added, sounding stupid but feeling like the distinction was important. She changed the subject.

"How are Vivian and Doris?" Molly was astounded to hear those names roll off her tongue—Charley's sisters, whom she hadn't thought of in more than 30 years.

"Well, Vivian is—"

He was interrupted by solemn music that heralded the beginning of the service. Molly glanced at her watch. "It's time to go in."

"Ohmygosh. Yeah. Well, anyhoo. Molly, can I call you sometime? We can have lunch and catch up."

He followed her into the chapel and slid into the pew beside her. As soon as they were seated, he fished in his pocket and came out with a scrap of paper and the stub of a pencil, which he handed to Molly. *What the hell,* she thought as she wrote down her phone number. The inappropriateness

44

of the situation was not lost on her. *But damn! Life was uncertain.* And Charley thought she was beautiful.

Chapter 12

Two days after Paul's funeral, Charley called.

"Hey, Molly. How ya doin', girl? I wanted to see if we could get together this weekend. Catch a movie. Get a bite to eat. Whatever you want."

"Charley? It sounds like there's traffic in the background. I can barely hear you."

"Oh, yeah, omygosh, well I'm on a pay phone."

"A pay phone?"

"Yeah, well, I'm out here on 40 Highway picking up some stuff for the tractor."

"You have a tractor?"

"Well, it's actually...hey, how about Friday night? Dinner?"

"Friday night?" Molly hesitated just long enough to give the impression she was considering her options. "Okay. What time?"

"Ohmygosh, let's see. How's about I pick you up at 6? You like Outback? They don't take reservations but we can do call-ahead seating."

Wow, Molly thought, *Outback. That's a definite step up from Best Burgers.* She listened to traffic noises while Charlie fumbled for a pen and something to write her address on. "Do you need directions?" she asked, "or will you do a MapQuest?"

Charlie said, "Uhm, better give me directions."

~~

"Charlie Hickman? Old Ichabod Crane! No kidding?"

Liz had been out of town over the weekend and Molly had just phoned to bring her up to date.

"You obviously remember him," she said.

46

"Sure. Tall, skinny guy. Married your cousin, Ginger. He had a couple of sisters who hung around with all of us. Back when you were married to Carl."

"That's him. God, Liz, we sound like an inbred bunch, don't we?"

"Not yet. Depends on whether he's still married to Ginger and what you intend to do with him. So...you said you gave him your phone number. Has he called?"

"This morning. And you know good and well he's not still married to Ginger. He's taking me out to dinner on Friday, to Outback Steak House. My fortunes are improving."

"For sure," Liz said. "I'll expect a full report. Take notes if you have to."

~~

That was Monday. There was a letter from Charlie in her mailbox on Tuesday afternoon. Molly opened it, expecting some lame excuse about why he wasn't going to show up Friday. How demoralizing —to get a *Dear Jane* letter before the first date.

But the letter read more like a resume.

Dear Molly,

Thank you for saying you'd go out with me. I'm really excited about taking you out. I guess you'd like to know more about where I'm at these days. Like I told you Saturday, I got married twice more after Ginger. I've been divorced for five years. I don't have a girlfriend. I don't drink or smoke or do drugs. I work part-time for a farmer with a lot of property between Grandview and Belton.

I get $1408 a month from Social Security, $575.00 a month from Teamsters and $135.36 from G.M. I'm not well-educated but I'm interested in what goes on in the world. I listen to NPR, watch public television and the History and Science Channels and spend a lot of time at the library. I don't know if politics matters to you, but

*I'm a Democrat. Well, anyhoo, I guess that's enough for
now. You can ask me anything else you want to know
Friday. I'm very open and honest.*

   Sincerely,

Charlie

Molly laid the letter on her kitchen table, smoothed it out
and read it again. It was written in a large, loopy scrawl on a
sheet from a yellow legal pad. It had been folded several
times to fit inside a 3-1/2 by 6-1/2 white envelope. She shook
her head. Was this some kind of strange courting ritual for
seniors? Get all the pertinent details out in the open right away?
Cut to the chase, we're not getting any younger?

She started to call Liz, but changed her mind. She wasn't
quite ready for Liz to make fun of him. She wasn't sure how
she felt herself. Granted, you couldn't accuse Charlie of being
suave. On the other hand, there was something endearing
about his guilelessness and lack of sophistication.

Chapter 13

The doorbell rang at five minutes till six. Molly jumped as if she hadn't been expecting it. She opened the door. Charlie stepped inside, amid a cloud of Aqua Velva that stung her eyes. He wore brown corduroy pants and a plaid shirt in shades of brown and tan. His boots were the same ones she had seen him in at the funeral.

A plastic grocery bag hung from the wrist of his left hand, which clutched a colorful bouquet of flowers. In his right hand he held an egg carton.

All Molly could think of to say was, "Wow, Charlie. What have you brought me?"

"Ohmygosh, Molly. You look gorgeous. And your house is beautiful. You must be rich. And, uh anyhoo...here." He thrust the flowers toward her and she heard something clink inside the plastic bag.

She took the flowers and said, "Well, come on in. I'll put these in some water." Charlie followed her to the kitchen. Molly watched in fascination as he set the egg carton on the table and slid the plastic bag off his wrist.

"I didn't know whether you liked red or white," he said as he pulled first a green bottle then a burgundy colored one from the bag. At first she thought it was wine but...

Molly laid the flowers on the table, picked up the green bottle and read the label. *Welch's Sparkling White Grape, Non-Alcoholic*. The label on the burgundy bottle said *Sparkling Red Grape, Non-Alcoholic*. In other words, glorified grape juice. Wow!

She lifted the lid on the egg carton and beheld a dozen small brown eggs. "Charlie," she said, "do you live on a farm?"

"Not exactly. I've got a trailer on a small patch of ground. The farmer I work for lets me keep my trailer there free. And

49

I've got a little garden and some chickens. Anyhoo, I thought you'd like to have some fresh eggs, right off the nest."

"Why thank you. Go in the living room and sit while I put these things away." Molly herded him through the door and around the corner to a couch at the far end of the living room.

She returned to the kitchen, sat at the table and stared at her bounty. It occurred to her that she might be overdressed for this date, in her soft emerald green pantsuit and silver sandals, which Dennis had approved from the cruise purchases.

When Molly emerged from the kitchen, Charlie asked to use her phone to call ahead for seating. Then he took her arm and led her out to his car. It was an early 90s model red Escort station wagon with a cracked windshield on the passenger side. He opened the door for her. When she started to get in, he stopped her.

"Oh, wait. Ohmygosh, I should have done this before I left." He reached past her, picked up a Pepsi can, a crumpled Wendy's sack and a paper cup from the floorboard and tossed them over the seat into the back.

Just when Molly thought he was finished, he said, "Oops, wait." He plucked a French fry off the console and tossed it into the back, then straightened to his full six feet and stood aside.

As she got in, Molly glanced into the back of the vehicle. The back of the seat had been folded down to create cargo space all the way to the rear window. Besides the fast-food refuse, there were a couple of baseball caps, a straw hat, an empty motor oil can and what looked like clumps of hay. The smell reminded her of barn mice.

~~~

Even though Charlie had called ahead, they had to wait nearly half an hour for a table. Charlie declined the hostess's offer to seat them at the bar while they waited.

Their table turned out to be a booth large enough for six people.

A perky waitress in denim shorts and a tight tee bounced up to the booth and chirped, "Hi, I'm Sandy and I'll be your server this evening." She recited the specials, indicated the menus at the end of the table and asked, "What can I get you to drink while you decide?"

Charlie ordered iced tea. Molly longed for something stronger, but the thought of the sparkling grape juice made her consider the possibility that Charlie was a recovering alcoholic. She ordered coffee. As she studied the menu, Molly felt Charlie staring at her. She looked up.

"Umm, so what do you think, Molly? I know this is a steak house, but they really do a good job on chicken. I think that's what I'm having."

Molly sighed and closed the menu. "Sounds great, Charlie. I'll have whatever you're having."

Charlie turned out to be a talker. He was surprisingly well informed about local, national and world affairs. While they were on the same page politically, it was obvious that he analyzed at a far deeper level than she did. He really got wound up during his discussion of the energy crisis. He shoved his hand in his pants pocket and came out with a crumpled invoice from National Tractor Equipment. He moved dishes aside, spread out the invoice and turned it over. Using the pen their waitress had left with the bill, he drew a rough outline he said was the Soviet Union.

"See, here's the problem. Russia is sitting on the biggest natural reserves of gas and oil in the world. And down here," he sketched in a few squiggles she couldn't identify, "is the part of the world we're worried about. Now compare the size." He poked at his map. "Who do you think America should be worryin' about?" He leaned back in his seat, cryptic and triumphant.

Molly said, "Excuse me, Charlie. I need to find the ladies' room."

~~

"Thanks for dinner, Charlie. And...everything." Molly had her keys in her hand when Charlie pulled into her driveway. She opened the passenger door and turned to him.

"I'd ask you in for coffee but I'm really not feeling well. I'm afraid something didn't agree with me."

"Gee, Molly. I'm sorry. Well, uhm, anyhoo, I'll call you."

He waited until she opened her door and turned on a light before he pulled out of the drive.

Chapter 14

Molly listened to Liz's voice on the answering machine while she rummaged through the cabinet under the sink, until she found a bottle of Johnny Walker Red that had been there for God only knows how long.

Molly, how was your date? Call me as soon as you get home, no matter what time it is. Joe went to the lake and I'll be up. So call, even if it's late. Okay?

She put several ice cubes in a tumbler, added a smidgen of water, topped it off with scotch and carried it to the living room.

As she leaned back in her recliner and felt the scotch burn her throat, warm her stomach and loosen her limbs, she kicked off her sandals and wiggled her toes. She made short work of the drink and padded into the kitchen in her bare feet for a refill. She returned to the recliner, took a long drink and reviewed the evening.

She thought about how she had agonized over what to wear and how she had finally been satisfied with the way she looked. "And I should have been satisfied 'cause I looked gooood!" she told herself as she drained the glass. "Don' know why I bothered, though." She reached for the phone. Liz answered on the first ring.

"Well?"

"Liz, why does God hate me?"

"Honey, I'm sure She doesn't. I'll be there in 20 minutes. Don't drink any more of whatever you're drinking until I get there."

Nineteen and a half minutes later, Liz arrived in her nightclothes and let herself in with her own key. A faded blue chenille robe, belt untied, hung open to reveal pajamas with a

53

pattern of moons, stars and sleeping cows. A pair of pink plastic flip-flops completed the ensemble.

Molly sat at the table and watched Liz bustle around her kitchen. The first thing she did, at Molly's insistence, was fix a scotch and water for herself and another for Molly. Next, she started a pot of coffee brewing then sat down across the table from Molly.

"Okay, tell me everything. Are those from him?" she asked, nodding at the flowers Molly had unceremoniously jammed into a water glass without bothering to arrange them.

"Yes, and that's not all." Molly sighed and took a sip of her drink. She noticed it wasn't nearly as strong as the first two had been. "He also brought me a dozen eggs and two bottles of non-alcoholic wine."

"Non-alcoholic wine? Isn't that some kind of an oxymoron?" Liz asked.

"Not in Charlie's world, I guess. Let me show you." She got up, opened the refrigerator and pulled out the two bottles and the carton of eggs and set them on the counter. She lifted the lid on the egg carton and said, "And eggs, see? Fresh from the nest."

Liz picked up one of the eggs. "Actually, it looks like it's fresh from the chicken's ass. He didn't bother to wash them, did he?"

"He told me he doesn't drink," Molly mused, "which explains the grape juice. And he has some chickens and a garden, which explains the eggs. The flowers are normal. So, is he just a big goofy country boy trying to be nice, Liz? Or what?"

"Well, my guess is he was hoping to disarm you with the flowers, seduce you with grape juice and stay over for a three-egg omelet."

She took the eggs to the sink, covered them with warm water, threw the carton away and washed her hands. Then she poured two cups of coffee and sat back down. "Let's hear the rest of it," she said.

Molly started with the letter then took up the story at the point where Charlie arrived for their date.

By the time Molly was finished, Liz had dished up two plates of fresh scrambled eggs and a stack of buttered toast. She refilled their coffee cups and dug in. "Okay, Molly," she said around a mouthful of farm fresh scrambled eggs, "let's talk about how you're going to get rid of Charlie. And why you should."

Chapter 15

Charlie called around noon Saturday. "Hey, Molly, girl. How ya doin'? You were a little green around the gills when I dropped you off last night. Anyhoo, I was worried about you and I'm calling to see if you're okay."

Molly thought, *Aw, that's sweet*. Then Liz popped into her head, shaking a finger at her, and her thought turned to *Aw, crap*.

She said, "Thanks for the concern, Charlie. I'm better, but still not great."

"It surely wasn't something you ate at Outback. We both had the same thing and I'm fine as frog hair. In fact, I wondered if you'd like to catch a movie this afternoon."

"I'm afraid I can't," Molly said. "I plan to lie around and recover for a couple of days. Then," she went on, thinking fast, "I've got a busy schedule this month. My son is getting married in a few days and I'm really swamped."

"Ohmygosh, well I guess I won't bother you, then. Anyhoo, I'll call you in a couple of weeks. Don't forget about me."

Why didn't she just come out and tell him not to call again, she wondered, as she hung up the phone? Putting it off wouldn't make it any easier and she was sure she hadn't heard the last of Charlie. He wasn't going to be as easy to get rid of as Bob had been.

The thought of Bob prompted her to go check her Senior Matchmaker account. She had checked it every day since the disastrous so called date, halfway expecting to get a nasty message from him.

If she was going to hear from him, this would probably be the day, she thought as she went to turn on her computer, right in keeping with the rest of her day.

You have a message.

She was so certain the message would be from Bob (or Beau) that it took her a moment to shift gears.

It read: *Is that you, Molly? G.P.*

Oh, my God. Who is G.P. and how does he know my name? How could this happen? This site is supposed to protect my identity.

It couldn't be Bob. She didn't know his last name, but his first initial should be B for Bob or Beau or R for Robert. *Who is G.P.?*

She recalled Dennis saying he sent the article about Internet dating to his dad, too. Gil. Gil Parker. But how would he know?

Then she remembered how they had gotten on the subject of crossword puzzles over dessert the other night. Gil laughingly admitted his fondness for them was equaled only by his ineptitude. That's when Richie had boasted that, "Mom's so cocky, she works them in ink."

Was that enough to make Gil guess she was Dreamcatcher? Well, that and where she lived and physical description and what else? Attitude. When she added that line to her profile— the one about working crosswords in ink, her thought had been to discourage some of the illiterates on the site. Oh, my God. How embarrassing. What should she do?

Ignore it! She closed the site and shut down the computer.

She went to the kitchen counter, picked up her grocery list in progress and reviewed it. She added clean, white eggs and real wine and left for the store.

Chapter 16

Molly came out of HyVee with a cart full of groceries to find her driver's side rear tire flat.

"Shit, shit, shit. I'm *so* ready for this fucking day to be over!" she fumed. Hands on hips, she studied the flat tire, shaking her head. She unlocked the car and loaded the groceries into the back seat, and then jammed the cart into the nearest return stall.

"I don't have time for this shit," she muttered as she stomped back to her car. She hit the remote to pop the trunk and pulled up the heavy cover that concealed the spare tire. "Damn! What the fuck am I supposed to do with this little baby tire? And this jumble of shit in the middle that I presume is supposed to get transformed into a fucking jack?" It dawned on Molly that she was thinking out loud about the same time she felt she was being watched.

"Need some help?"

He drew a long leg over the motorcycle he'd been sitting on and walked toward her.

"That's okay. I'll call someone." She plucked her cell phone out of a small side pocket of her handbag and flipped it open. Then she stood there staring stupidly at the phone wondering who to call.

"You could do that," he said. "But I could have it fixed before anyone gets here—and before your ice cream melts." His voice was deep and lazy, almost to the point of being insolent.

"What makes you think I have any ice cream in there?"

"Just a hunch." He gestured toward the trunk and she moved aside.

He had the jack assembled in nothing flat. He lifted out the bubble tire and checked that it was inflated. Molly watched his practiced movements. He worked quickly and efficiently, without conversation. Once, he looked up and caught her watching him. He slid his sunglasses down and stared at her so long she felt uncomfortable. She was the first one to shift her gaze.

When he went back to tightening the lug nuts on the little spare, she studied him. He wore black jeans and a sleeveless black shirt—Molly thought it was called a muscle shirt—appropriately so as she could see his muscles flex with each turn of the tire tool. His black boots had studded straps over the tops. His salt and pepper hair hung down his back in a braid.

When he finished tightening the lug nuts, he stood up and put everything, including the flat tire, back in the trunk and slammed the lid.

"That should hold you 'til you can get it fixed or replaced."

"You're certainly a fast worker!" Molly said. "I don't know how to thank you."

He pulled off the sunglasses and looked at her again. It was a long, bold look that just bordered on offensive.

"Well! Okay, then," Molly stammered. "Here, let me pay you." She reached into her bag and pulled out her wallet.

"I don't take money for helpin' a damsel in distress," he drawled, "even one that swears like a sailor."

As he turned and strode back to his motorcycle, she blushed at the thought that he had heard her little tirade.

She jammed her wallet back into her bag, got in her car and drove away. She was aware that he sat on his motorcycle and watched her pull out of the parking lot. She wasn't sure which she appreciated more, his changing her tire or the fact that he never once called her ma'am.

~~~

She was disciplined about deducting her debit card expenditures from her checkbook and that was her first thought after putting away the groceries. That was also when she discovered her wallet was missing.

She rummaged through the depths of her large handbag, pushing everything this way and that with a sinking feeling. She upended the bag and poured the contents out on the kitchen table. It wasn't there.

Neither was it in her car nor anywhere along the path from her car to the house. She fought down panic and tried to retrace her movements. She had it at HyVee when she took out her debit card to pay for the groceries. And she had taken it out of her bag when she offered to pay the guy who changed her tire. And she didn't have it now.

She drove back to the store and searched the parking lot where she had parked earlier. Nothing. She went inside and inquired if anyone had found it. No one had, but they would be sure and call her if it turned up.

Molly drove home filled with dread at the prospect of having to call all of her credit card companies, report the cards lost, get them replaced and replace her driver's license. How much cash was in the wallet? She figured there was at least $88. She had withdrawn money for her grandson's birthday. She felt sick.

When she turned onto her street and saw the motorcycle in her driveway, she couldn't begin to sort her thoughts. It was the guy from the HyVee parking lot. What was he doing here? He was sitting sideways on the big Harley with his arms crossed and a cigarette hanging from the corner of his mouth. No, not a cigarette —it was a piece of a plastic straw. She got out of her car cautiously, with her thumb on the panic button of her remote.

"Are you stalking me?"

He stood up and held out her wallet. "Are you leaving a trail— like a dropped hankie—for me to follow?"

"Oh, my God. You found my wallet." Molly's knees went weak with relief as her fingers closed around the precious object. "How can I...?" she trailed off, remembering the look in the parking lot when she asked how she could thank him. "How did you...?"

"Your address from your driver's license."

"It's not an easy one to find."

"I'm familiar with the neighborhood. My aunt and uncle live nearby."

"I can't tell you how relieved I am. It looks like I owe you another debt of gratitude." She cringed, wondering what he would make of that.

"No problem," he said. "You should go ahead and check that everything's still there. It is."

"Well, I really appreciate it. But I wonder. . . why didn't you just take it back in the store — or to the police?"

He took off the sunglasses and gave her a long look. "Then I couldn't get to know you."

"That's pretty presumptuous. What makes you think you're going to get to know me? What makes you think I don't have a husband in there?" She nodded toward the house.

"Just a hunch, Molly."

She was startled to hear him say her name.

"I'm Harvey Holcombe." His eyes never left hers. "My friends call me Hoot."

He threw a long leg over the motorcycle and stomped on the starter.

The big Harley roared to life. Molly felt the vibration through the soles of her shoes. She clutched her wallet to her breast and watched him ride away. Her thumb was still on the panic button of her remote.

Inside, she sat at the table and checked the contents of her wallet. Everything was there, including the credit cards and $88. Tucked between her driver's license and her library card was a page ripped from a small note book. The handwriting was bold with generous ascenders and descenders.

Let's get acquainted. Call me. Hoot. 547-1147.

Like that's about to happen, Molly thought. *You didn't take anything from my wallet, but that doesn't mean you're not dangerous.* She tossed the note into the basket on the counter where she kept unpaid bills. She vaguely wondered why she hadn't thrown it in the trash.

Chapter 17

Molly glanced at the caller ID, saw it was Gil, and thought about not answering the phone. She felt her face flush at the memory of that "Is that you, Molly" message.

Damn! She couldn't avoid him. He'd be here soon for the wedding. Well, she would just deny everything. She picked up the receiver. "Hello."

"Hi, Molly. It's Gil. I hope this isn't a bad time."

"Not at all, Gil. Are you ready to head for Missouri again?"

"I am. And I want to thank you for inviting me to stay at your house this trip. That was very thoughtful of you."

"It just makes sense," Molly said. "You won't have to sit around a motel room between events and more importantly, you won't have to put up with a couple of gay guys getting crazy with the wedding jitters. And you won't have to worry about finding your way around. You can ride with me to the wedding and reception and everything."

"I can't tell you how much I appreciate it," Gil said. "I'll try not to get in your way."

"I'm sure it won't be a problem. Who's picking you up at the airport?"

"Dennis. I should be at your house around one o'clock Friday."

"Great. I'll see you then."

She hung up and blew out a sigh of relief. He hadn't said a word about Senior Matchmakers.

Chapter 18

Molly pulled fresh linens onto the bed in the guestroom when the phone rang. She rushed to the kitchen and picked it up on the third ring.

A deep voice said, "It's been three days. I guess you're not gonna call me." When she didn't reply, he added, "This is Hoot."

"How did you get my phone number?" she demanded. "From the phonebook."

"You're starting to scare me. What do you want?"

"I want to get acquainted with you."

"I'm afraid that's not going to happen," Molly said.

"Can we talk about it?"

"There's nothing to talk about. And I really don't have time for this. I'm getting ready for a wedding this weekend."

"Please don't tell me you're gettin' married."

Molly burst out laughing. "Not me. It's my son." She wondered why she didn't just slam the phone down and end this ridiculous exchange. She remembered Hoot's eyes and the bold way he had stared at her. She needed to snap out of it.

"Actually," she said, prolonging the conversation almost against her will, "you may as well know it's my son and his gay partner. I'm sure you don't want to get acquainted with me. My son's alternate lifestyle isn't the only thing that makes this family a little different — make that a lot different."

"If you're tryin' to scare me off, it's not workin'. I don't judge other people's lifestyles."

"Hoot, I'm flattered, but I'm really busy. I have a guest coming from out-of-town for the wedding. And I have a million things to do."

"That's the first time you've said my name."

"I'm hanging up now," Molly said.

Hoot said, "I'll call you next week."

"It won't do you . . ." There was a click, cutting the connection ". . . any good," she finished, with a sigh.

Chapter 19

Dennis arrived with Gil a few minutes before 1 o'clock Friday after noon. He carried Gil's suitcase to the guestroom, and rushed back out to the living room.

"Okay, Dad, I've got to run. I'm sorry to dump you so unceremoniously, but I have to meet with the photographer and I'm leaving you in good hands."

He grabbed Molly and gave her a big hug.

"Mollymoms, thanks for babysitting the old man. I love you both. I'll see you tomorrow." And he was gone.

Molly said, "Would you like a cup of coffee?"

"Sounds great," Gil said.

He leaned against the kitchen archway while she poured the coffee and set a small pitcher of cream next to the sugar bowl.

She watched him doctor his coffee and said, "Please, go on in the living room and make yourself at home. I'm going to finish unloading the dishwasher and then I'll join you."

She emerged from the kitchen a few minutes later to find Gil studying the family photos that took up most of both walls in the hallway.

She flipped on the hall light. "I finally got around to taking out the old ones and replacing them with the latest I have of everyone," she said. "Just this week, in fact."

"How about a guided tour?" Gil asked.

"Okay, but let me know when you've had enough. It can be pretty dull, looking at pictures of people you don't know."

"Not at all. I'm hoping it will give me a head start remembering who's who at the wedding."

Molly started with the first group. "This is my oldest, Sophie, and her husband, Myron and their two boys — Gus, 12 and Zach, 9.

Gil smiled. "No sissy names for them."

"You noticed. However, I think Sophie is getting nervous about them. Gus is a little smartass who corrects his teacher's grammar, and reads the opinion page of the newspaper. And the other day, he wrote a letter to the editor complaining about the president's inability to pronounce nuclear. They're both brilliant, but I'm sure Sophie would be happier if they were more interested in some sort of contact sports."

They moved to the next picture. "Of course you recognize these two." She stopped in front of the 8x10 of Dennis standing behind Richie, his hand resting on Richie's shoulder.

"Yes, they sent me the same picture, same frame even," Gil said.

"And these are Sam's children and grandchildren." Molly was preparing to name them when Gil turned to the opposite wall and the holiday photo of Molly and Sam.

"How long has he been gone?"

"A little over two years," Molly said.

Gil turned from the picture and looked at Molly. "It must be hard, losing two husbands."

"Technically, I've lost three," Molly said, "but Sam is the only one I ever missed."

Gil raised a questioning eyebrow.

"This is probably TMI, as the grandkids say—too much information. But here it is. I got married the first time when I was 19 to Carl. He left me after four years because I was barren. As far as I know, he's not dead.

"My kids' dad, Frank, died six years after we were divorced. He left because he was an asshole. He couldn't accept what Richie was turning into, as he put it. And Sam didn't want to leave me but nobody asked him." Molly was aware of the bitterness that had crept into her voice and felt a little embarrassed.

Gil was quiet for a moment. Then, "Molly," he said, "at the risk of being way too nosy, I have to ask. You said your first husband, Carl, left you because you were barren. That sort of calls for an explanation."

"I think there are a couple of cups of coffee left," she said, and led the way to the kitchen.

"Carl came from a big family." She took another mug from the cupboard, filled it and refilled Gil's mug.

"Five sisters and two brothers. They were all reproducing like a warren of rabbits. When I didn't get pregnant within the first year, Carl and his entire family panicked. His mom called me at least once a week with questions and advice. Was I praying for a child? Had I tried eating raw eggs? She even had helpful suggestions about the positions I should assume, during and after what she primly referred to as our conjugating."

Gil choked on his coffee. "Was she talking about sex or verbs?"

Molly grinned. "You wouldn't believe how many times I bit my tongue, but the woman wouldn't have known a verb from a noun. Anyhow, Carl got more frustrated every time one of his siblings had another baby, which was disgustingly often. It never once occurred to anyone in his family that it might be his fault, not mine. The one time I mentioned the possibility to Carl, he got drunk and didn't come home for three days."

Gil asked, "So were you surprised to find out you and Frank were expecting?"

"A little. And a funny thing happened about Carl. Mom and Dad ran into him at a Swap and Shop about six years after we were divorced. He was with a young gal he introduced as his wife and was proudly pushing a baby boy around in a stroller. Mom made over the baby like she did with all babies. Then she said, 'He sure is cute. Looks just like his mommy.'

"Dad gleefully reported to Carl that I had remarried and had two children. When they told me about it later, Mom said she really *couldn't* see that the little boy looked anything like Carl. Dad said he couldn't tell, that all babies looked alike to him. He said if you asked him, somebody had it in for old Carl."

Gil laughed. "Your dad sounds like someone I'd have liked to meet."

"He was a great guy and quite a character. I'll never get over missing him and Mom. They died within six months of each other, Mom first, then Dad. I think he died of grief."

After a moment, she continued, "I know he didn't starve to death because widows for miles around beat a path to his door with casseroles and baked goods."

Gil chuckled. "I can relate to that. I got a lot of casseroles and cakes after Dennis's mom died." He rose and took both of their empty cups to the sink and rinsed them. Molly was still marveling at this little, seemingly unconscious act of domesticity, when Gil came back to the table and sat down. She watched him trace a pattern on the place mat with his forefinger.

After a few moments of silence, he looked at her searchingly and said, "Molly, when did you first notice something different about Richie?"

She considered the question. "Well, he seemed really curious about some of Sophie's toys. She had a trunk full of stuff for dress up, discarded purses and high heels, jewelry, boas and so forth. Richie was intrigued with those things and liked to handle them. But I wasn't too worried until one day I walked out of the house and saw him barreling down the sidewalk on his tricycle with an old purse hanging on the handlebar, a pair of high heels dangling off his feet and a candy cigarette hanging from the corner of his mouth. He looked like a little gun moll with a crew cut. I'd have to say that was when his life flashed before my eyes."

"So how did you handle it?"

"I tried to distract him. Then I tried to discuss it with Frank. Well, that was a mistake! He had a fit. He screamed at me, 'How'd he get to be this way? You'd better do something about him before it's too late. The last thing in the world I want to put up with is a queer son.'

"I didn't know as much about the subject as I do now, but even then I didn't think there was anything I could do to change Richie. And I knew there was nothing Richie could do to make me not love him."

She felt a flush across her cheeks and the bridge of her nose, and took a deep breath to drive back the threat of tears.

Gil said, "Richie and Dennis had a lot in common. They each had a parent who couldn't deal with their difference."

Molly looked at him, surprised. She saw deep pain in his eyes. "I'm sorry," she said. "I didn't know." Then as an afterthought, she blurted, "Oh, no. Was it you?"

"Let's go for a walk and I'll tell you about it. Is there someplace to walk around here that doesn't involve a quarter mile paved oval?"

"There are some great nature trails in Blue Springs, just down I-70 a few miles. Better put on your sneakers. My favorite trail is a little challenging."

"Sounds like just what I need," Gil said and went to change. He emerged from the guestroom wearing blue jeans with a crisp crease, a navy blue cotton polo and a pair of white cross trainers. Molly felt a tad underdressed in her faded jeans that hadn't seen a crease since she could remember.

She took him to Burr Oak Woods in Blue Springs. Gil was pensive during the drive and didn't seem inclined to get back to the conversation. Molly parked at the mouth of the Bethany Falls trail. She turned to Gil.

"Before we start, let me say I don't usually go into the woods with men I barely know." She was joking.

"And let me say it wasn't me who couldn't deal with Dennis's difference." He was serious.

Chapter 20

A short way into the woods the trail forked. "Let's go this way," Molly said, leading the way to the right. "I'd rather climb up the rock formations ahead than try to look graceful coming down them."

They walked in silence for several minutes before Gil began to speak. "I could have accepted that Louise and I made a mistake in marrying each other. And it was as much my fault as hers, maybe more."

"You're saying there were problems that didn't have anything to do with Dennis?"

"Oh, yeah." After a long pause, he went on. "I was 27 when we met, and she was 23. She was sweet, innocent, demure and proper. I thought her prudishness was charming. I assumed she was playing hard to get. And I, man of the world that I considered myself, was willing to marry her to get her."

"That's what all of us good girls did back then," Molly said. "We played hard to get. We truly believed our moms when they preached the old adage, why buy the cow if the milk's free."

As they crossed a wooden bridge over a small stream, Gil stopped and leaned on the railing.

"It turned out she wasn't *playing* hard to get," he said, gazing at the water below. "She *was* hard to get. Our first week of marriage was a disaster, with her constantly in tears and me constantly trying to figure out how to please her. We finally settled into a routine that seemed to work. She suffered my attentions dutifully and without enthusiasm and I was as clinical and unobtrusive as one can be and still get the job done."

Molly smiled. "Gil, I have to say I've never heard a less exciting description of sex. You *are* talking about sex. Right?"

"Right." Gil turned his head and met Molly's eyes. "It's hard not to talk about it in clinical terms. That's how I remember it. Anyway, we were both ready to call it quits by the end of the first year."

Molly leaned over the rail and watched a leaf zigzag through the bubbling water as Gil continued.

"But then she discovered she was pregnant. It was a difficult pregnancy and a difficult delivery. When it was over, Louise made it abundantly clear she would not go through that again. It was either total abstinence or vasectomy. At first I chose abstinence while I considered a third option—divorce. But then another love came into my life—our son. So I stayed and underwent the knife."

He straightened and they continued across the bridge.

"Louise took to motherhood a lot better than she had to being a wife. That is until she began to notice that Dennis wasn't like other little boys. He didn't care about trucks and tanks and toy soldiers, but he wanted to help bake cookies. He didn't like to get dirty and he constantly arranged and rearranged his room. And he was fussy, if not downright prissy, about his clothes."

"Do you think she understood what was going on?" Molly asked.

"Finally. She understood but didn't accept. It became her life's mission to straighten him out, make him normal. When he was about 8, she got worried because he was spending too much time with a boy who liked the same kinds of things Dennis liked. So she did everything she could to sabotage the friendship.

"Then she was thrilled when he showed an interest in a little girl who moved in down the street—until she realized he was more interested in the girl's Suzie Homemaker oven than he was in the girl. That's when she tried to distract him with karate lessons."

Molly glanced at Gil. "That must have been frustrating for both of them and you as well," she said.

He turned and looked at her. "I know *you* know that's an understatement, Molly."

"Yes." She was becoming uncomfortable with Gil's intensity when the looming boulders offered a break. "Look, there are the rock formations just ahead. I know you're used to mountains, but these are interesting. Let me tell you about them."

She scrambled up the railroad ties that served as a stairway to the huge boulders. She waited for Gil to catch up, and began to share the local history.

"During the Civil War, Jesse James and the Younger Brothers used these rock outcrops for a hideout and to store ammunition. According to old-timers who lived around here, they were also used by the Kansas Jayhawkers and the Missouri Bushwhackers between border raids."

Gil hadn't given a single indication that he was impressed.

"You can read about it on the signs just ahead," she said. One of them tells how this area was covered by a shallow ocean a couple of million years ago."

They moved along through the huge boulders until they came to the first sign. Molly hesitated, expecting Gil to stop and read. But he simply stood and looked at her until she moved on.

Well, crap, she thought. *I know it's not Pike's Peak, but I thought it was fascinating.* She walked past the remaining signs as if they weren't there.

The trail emerged from the outcropping into an open field. A shadow moved across the tall grass and they looked up to see a hawk soaring close to the ground—so close they could distinguish the finger-like tips of its wings. They watched in awe for a moment, and then continued along the path as it wound around the edge of the field toward another footbridge.

There was a bench at the far end of the bridge. Gil sat down, elbows on his knees and studied his clasped hands. He began to speak as if there had been no interruption in his story.

I guess that's why he wasn't impressed with the scenery. He just wants to talk.

"Then you know what she did?"

72

"You mean Louise?" Molly sat down beside him on the bench.

"Yes. She forgave him on her deathbed. She said, 'Son, I forgive you.' "Dennis was sitting by her hospital bed, holding her hand. He said, 'Forgive me for what, Mom?'

"She said, 'For, you know, being the way you are.'"

"Oh, my God," Molly whispered.

"Dennis just sat there for a minute, and then he said, 'I see. Well, thanks, Mom.' He let go of her hand and left the room.

"I've never laid a hand on a woman in anger, but I have to tell you I wanted to slap her right on into eternity. Instead, I went after Dennis. Louise died alone while I comforted our sobbing son."

They sat in silence for several minutes. Finally, Molly said, "That would have scarred him for life. How has he managed to get past it?"

"It wasn't easy. It took over a year of counseling before Dennis could forgive her and understand that she loved him in spite of her inability to accept him as he was."

Molly didn't know what to say. Her heart ached for Dennis.

After several moments passed, Gil seemed to shake off the memory. He looked up at Molly with a shy smile, "I love the way Dennis calls you Mollymoms."

"Me, too," she said. *Why do I feel like Gil is about to go somewhere with this that I'm not ready for?* She gazed out across the field. "I love the relationship I have with Dennis. He is as dear to me as Richie is. But I hope he doesn't see me as a surrogate mother. It sounds like counseling helped him resolve his feelings about Louise. I'm sure Dennis understands that she loved him the best she knew how. And that is the way he should remember her."

She stood abruptly and started to walk away. Then she turned back and regarded Gil. "I'd hate for anything to change the easy, comfortable relationship I have with Dennis." She held his eyes until she felt sure he understood. Then she said, "We'd better get back to the house and scare up something for dinner. Tomorrow's going to be a busy day."

Chapter 21

Liz and her husband, Joe, left for the reception hall to greet guests as soon as the wedding was over, while Molly and Gil stayed behind for the photo session.

"If we can put people in outer space," Molly grumbled to Gil, "you'd think we could come up with a way to get this photography business done seamlessly and not keep guests waiting at the reception. Speaking of which—" She took her cell phone from her small handbag and dialed Liz. "How's it going there?"

"We've got it under control...Hold on, Molly. Hello, Linda. Joe, you remember Sam's daughter and granddaughter, I'm sorry, hon, I don't remember your name." Molly heard a surly, "It's Gwen."

"Okay, Molly, I'm back. What's up? Oops, hold on. Hi, Jan. Nice dress. Very, uhm, tropical. Joe, hold the fort a minute. Molly, I'm back. Damn good thing there isn't a bride, 'cause Jan obviously didn't get the memo that it's someone else's day to shine. And that little Gwen is a real snot."

"Liz, be nice. And remember, you don't know how to whisper."

Molly disconnected and shook her head. "God, I hope this doesn't take much longer. Liz is out of control."

"I'm sure she and Joe will handle things very capably," Gil said. "Or at least entertainingly, from what I've heard about Liz."

The photographer's assistant called out, "Parents? Let's have the parents now. I understand there's just one parent per groom? Okay, we can work with that."

Gil took Molly's arm and said, "Come on. Let's get it over with."

"Dad," the assistant directed, "let's have you stand beside your handsome son. Mom, you tuck yourself up next to your gorgeous offspring."

The assistant made several more adjustments.

"Mother of the groom, dear, tilt your head a trifle to the left. Gil, darling, tuck in a little closer to Dennis." He moved back to Gil and guided him into position with more hands-on than was probably necessary. He finally gave Gil's cummerbund a little pat and stood back to survey his work. He gave a thumbs-up to the photographer and said, "Okay, James, take one."

Obviously these guys were from the gay community. Who else could turn a wedding photo session into a Broadway production?

Forty-eight minutes later, the entire wedding party joined the guests at the reception. As Richie and Dennis made their entrance, the crowd stood and applauded and the band began to play "Always".

The groom and groom bowed to the guests and waltzed onto the dance floor. Dennis, being the taller, took the lead. Such effortless grace! They appeared to float across the floor.

Molly heard a little girl in a froth of pink whisper, "Wow! They could be on *Dancing with the Stars*."

Their song ended and the band began to play "You Light Up My Life". Richie took Molly's hand and danced her slowly around the floor then handed her off to Dennis. "I wondered how you'd handle that," she laughed.

"Well, Mollymoms, I'm sure Dad would have gamely gotten up and danced with me, but I decided to spare him. We wouldn't have been able to agree on who should lead."

Dennis kissed Molly's hand and bowed to her, then joined Richie at the table that held the wedding cake. Richie picked up a crystal goblet and rapped on it with a tiny silver fork. "May I have your attention, please?"

The guests quieted and focused on the newlyweds. "Dennis and I want to thank all of you for sharing this happy event with us. We decided to forgo the standard cutting of the cake ceremony."

Dennis interrupted, "You will not see us shove cake into each others' faces and ruin the tuxes."

"True," Richie continued. "Instead, we'll toast each other in front of this beautiful cake that our good friends Lois and Irene created. Isn't it fabulous?

"Behold." He made a graceful Vanna White-type gesture toward the topmost layer, which held two grooms, one with dark hair and the other blonde. The guests applauded their appreciation.

Molly swept her eyes over the crowd. She noticed Jan leaning against a pillar with her arms crossed. She was particularly resplendent in a wispy, floor-length Hawaiian-print skirt and skinny black top. Her ears dripped dangly silver earrings, which matched the necklace and chunky bracelet she wore; it showed off her deep tan, compliments of the cruise from which she had just returned.

Liz materialized and slipped her arm around Molly's waist in time to see Jan wiggle her fingers in a dainty wave.

"Skinny bitch," Molly muttered.

"Never mind her," Liz said. "I'll help you kill her later. Let's watch the toast."

The band played a snippet from a Broadway tune and a band member with a decent voice sang, "I want to be the first man you'll remember. I want to be the last man you'll forget," as the grooms toasted each other.

It wasn't long before the band picked up the pace and couples, both gay and straight, swarmed onto the floor. Gil handed Molly a glass of wine and sat down at the table with her, Liz and Joe. "Do you suppose all gay guys are great dancers?"

"It certainly seems that way," Molly answered.

Jan had made her way across the room and approached the table. She stuck her hand out to Gil and said, "You must be Dennis's dad. I'm Jan, Molly's sister-in-law. Her brother's widow," she added—unnecessarily— in Molly's opinion.

He stood and shook her hand. "Gil," he said. Glad to meet you. Would you like to join us?" He pulled a chair from another table.

"I'd love to." She sat down and looked around the table. "Hi, Liz, Joe. How's it going, Molly?" Without waiting for an answer, she turned to Gil. "Now tell me everything about yourself. Do you do much traveling?"

Joe got up and reached for Molly's hand. "Molly come and dance with a fat old man while they're playing a slow one."

As they merged onto the floor, he said, "Looks like Jan's moving in for the kill."

"I didn't think men paid attention to things like that," Molly smiled.

"Basic Liz training," he said. "She'll ask me if I noticed as soon as we're alone."

When they returned to the table, Liz grabbed Molly's arm before she could sit down and herded her to the ladies' room. "Jesus," she said as soon as the door closed. "It's like watching an episode of *Hunter and Hunted* on *National Geographic*. She's already asked him how long he's been a widower, how long he'll be in town, doesn't he hate living so far away from his son, blah, blah, blah. She's about as subtle as a dinner gong. Are you going to let her get away with that?"

"What am I supposed to do? Gil's a big boy. He can take care of himself. It's none of my business."

Liz narrowed her eyes and stepped way into Molly's personal space. "Go rescue him," she demanded, "or I'm going to be forced to make a scene."

"What if he doesn't want to be rescued?"

"Now," Liz said and stomped out of the ladies' room.

Molly slumped into the only chair in sight. *I'm not about to get into a catfight over some man I don't have any claim on. What am I supposed to do? Invite Jan to arm wrestle. Best three out of five. Winner gets the guy, whether he knows it or not? What does Liz want from me? Anyway, she won't really make a scene.*

Wait! It's Liz. Molly jumped up and rushed out the door, close on Liz's heels.

Jan was leaning in close to Gil and had her hand on his arm. Liz sat down next to her and eyed Jan's drink.

77

Oh, no. She's going to dump the drink on Jan, Molly thought. She hurried to the table and touched Gil on the shoulder.

"Gil, let me tear you away and introduce you to the children of the family."

"Sounds like fun." Gil stood and followed Molly. She felt Jan's piercing glare on her back.

A special table had been set up for the children toward the back of the hall. It was littered with paper plates smeared with frosting.

One of the bartenders kept the children supplied with soft drinks. The little girl in pink assumed a mature attitude as she sipped a Shirley Temple.

The oldest child at the table was Sam's granddaughter, Gwen, who slouched in her chair, boredom oozing from every pore. Molly and Gil approached the table, unnoticed, in time to hear Gwen say, "Hey y'all. I've been trying to figure out which one of them is the girl and which is the boy."

Molly stopped in her tracks.

"What do you mean?" asked Molly's grandson, Zach.

"You know," Gwen said. "Like who cooks and cleans and who takes care of the manly stuff? They both seem pretty sissified to me."

All the children's attention was focused on Gwen, except for the little girl in pink who only had eyes for her Shirley Temple. Molly started to move toward the table, but Gil held her back.

"It's not like that, Gwen," Zach spoke with authority. "They're not like boy and girl, like other couples. They're a different species."

"I think you mean gender," Gus said. "And they're actually both pretty good cooks."

"You mean you'd actually eat something they cooked?"

"Gwen," Molly said sharply enough to get their collective attention.

Gwen faced Molly and answered with an insolent, "Yeah?"

78

Molly took a deep breath. "This is Dennis's dad, Gil. Gil, this is my oldest granddaughter, Gwen."

"That's step-granddaughter," Gwen said. My real grandma, Granddad's first wife, lives in Wichita."

"How could I have forgotten?" Molly was shaking with fury. "Gwen, I don't think you really belong at the children's table. Why don't you go sit at the table with your Mom?"

"So gladly." Gwen grabbed her Coke and left in a huff.

Molly took a deep breath and turned to the table. "Gil, these are Sophie's boys. Gus is 12 and Zach is 9."

"How's it going, guys?" He shook hands with each of them.

"These are Sammy Jr.'s girls, my granddaughters, Samantha and Crystal. Girls, tell Gil how old you are so I don't get it wrong and embarrass myself."

"Glad to meet you, sir," Samantha said. "I'm 12."

"Me, too," Crystal said. "I mean me, too, glad to meet you, not me, too, I'm 12. She giggled. "I'm 10, going on 11."

"It's a good thing Grandma Molly has us," Samantha said. "Otherwise, she wouldn't have any granddaughters."

"That's right, Grandma," Crystal said. "You don't even need old snotty Gwen. Can we un-adopt her and Aunt Linda from the family?"

Molly swallowed hard and bent to hug each of them. She turned to the little girl in pink. "Honey, I don't know your name."

"I'm Thylvia," she answered with a shy lisp.

"And who did you come here with, Sylvia?"

"My mommies, the cake ladies."

"Well, I'm honored to be in such lovely company," Gil said. He took each girl's hand and repeated the corresponding name flawlessly.

I'll bet he'll be able to call all of them by name a week from now, Molly thought, *and I'll be lucky if I can remember Sylvia the rest of the day.*

Molly turned from the children's table to see Jan charging across the room.

"Gil! Oh, Gil! There you are! I wanted to say good-bye. I'm leaving before the party gets any crazier. Liz is already

79

on the dance floor in her stocking feet doing the electric slide with a couple of the gay guys. Oops, sorry." She clamped her hand over her mouth and glanced at the children's table. "Forget I said that."

"Oh, no," Gus exclaimed. He leaned back in his chair and slapped his forehead. "The truth's out now. There are gays in our midst."

There were giggles and snorts all around the table, except from Sylvia, who just smiled and took a dainty sip from her Shirley Temple.

Gil chuckled, Molly tried not to laugh and Jan turned red under her tan. She said, "Oh, Gus, you're just too clever." The smile on her lips didn't quite reach her eyes. Gil, I'll give you a call at Molly's tomorrow. Maybe we can go out to lunch and continue our conversation." And she was gone in a swish of Hawaiian print and a jangle of silver.

Molly watched Gil watch her leave. She wondered what he was thinking and what the conversation was that Jan wanted to continue. She was suddenly exhausted and wanted nothing more than for this day to be over.

Chapter 22

"My feet are killing me." Molly kicked off her shoes the minute she was through the door. "Gil, you'll have to excuse me while I slip into something more comfortable. And by comfortable, I mean my grubbies."

"Good idea," Gil said. "Enough of the formal attire. I hear my jeans calling from the suitcase."

Molly breathed a separate sigh of relief with each article of clothing she peeled off...dress, slip, pantyhose. She was tempted to jettison her bra, too, and would have if she had been alone. She pulled on a pair of faded cropped pants and a big tee shirt and went to join Gil.

She found him on the deck with a couple of glasses of iced tea. He had changed into a different pair of jeans from the ones he wore yesterday, and a blue houndstooth shirt, with the sleeves rolled up and the first couple of buttons undone. A thatch of curly gray hair was visible in the vee left by the open buttons. *Must be nice to be a man and not have to think twice about baring one's chest.* She was amused to see he was barefoot, too.

Gil handed her a glass of iced tea and sat in one of the chairs, leaving the chaise lounge for her. A gentle breeze blew across the deck. Molly leaned back in the chaise and sighed. "My God, it feels good to sit. Gil, you're about to find out what a rotten hostess I am because I'm about to tell you I'm not moving to fix you any dinner. I don't know what you'll do if you can't make yourself a sandwich. My feet refuse to move." She wiggled her toes and took a drink of tea.

"I know exactly what to do," Gil said. "I'll look up the number for pizza delivery and open a couple of beers." He set his glass on the wrought iron table and scooted his chair close to the chaise. "I'll even serve, and your feet won't have to move." He took her right foot in his hands and began to massage it.

"Wow, where did you come from? And what have I done to deserve this? Bad hostess that I am—refusing to feed you?" Molly realized she was babbling.

"You deserve it for spending the day in high-heels. No wonder your feet are killing you. I'm not sure when it was decided that high-heels weren't attractive on men, but I'm eternally grateful." He switched his attention to her left foot. "I'm also sensitive to the injustice of it all. So enjoy."

As she closed her eyes and gave in to the sensation, she thought, *eat your heart out, Jan.*

After he had thoroughly massaged both of her feet, Gil pushed back his chair and picked up his tea. "Wasn't it a great wedding and reception? Everything came off without a hitch— no pun intended."

Molly smiled. "Yes, except for the near-altercation with Sam's granddaughter. I can't tell you how happy I am that she and her mother decided to drive back to Wichita this afternoon instead of spending the night—even though I invited them to stay."

"I'm glad, too." He stood and stretched. "Now what would you like on your pizza?"

~~

They decided to eat in the kitchen to avoid sharing their food with the flies that had started to bite. A sure sign it was going to rain. And rain it did—in sheets. They sat at the kitchen table, eating pizza and sipping cold beer, and watched the storm through the sliding glass doors.

When they finished, Molly insisted on clearing the table, "Since you've done everything else," she told Gil.

He wandered into the living room and studied her extensive collection of CDs until she joined him.

"Is all of this your music, Molly? I mean not left over from your kids?"

"Yes, it's all mine. Why do you ask?"

"It's just—well—you have quite an eclectic taste in music. You've got classical, country, new age, big band. And what's this?" He chuckled as he read, *Dr. Hook, Sloppy Seconds.*

Molly felt herself blush, remembering the titles of some of the cuts on that one. "I had to buy that to get one song that wasn't on his Greatest Hits album."

"I see. Hmmm." He scanned the titles and raised an eyebrow in mock disapproval. "And to think I let my kid hang out with your kid."

She crossed the room and took the CD out of his hand. "See, it's number seven. I bought it for number seven."

Gil was pulling out another jewel case. "Wow! Eddy Arnold. I haven't thought about him in years. I'm surprised you've got him on a CD."

"Well, once again, I bought it for a particular song—"Molly Darling". Not because I felt like it was my song or anything. It's because of my grandma Molly. I'm named after her. She used to tell me about how grandpa sang it to her. I got to thinking about it a couple of years ago and went looking for it on the Internet. It's pretty corny and old-fashioned. But I like to think about him trying to win her over by singing to her. She was kind of a spitfire. I understand she slapped him and called him a son-of-a-bitch the first time he kissed her."

Gil smiled. "I'd like to have met her. Can I hear the song?"

"Okay, but promise you won't make fun of it. It's really schmaltzy but I'm sensitive about it." She took the disc from the case, put it on the player and selected number nine.

Eddy Arnold's smooth voice sang, *Won't you tell me Molly darling. . . that you'll love none else but me. . .*

Gil listened for a moment, and then held out his hand to Molly. "May I have this dance?" He was smiling, but she didn't think he was making fun of her...yet.

They began to move to the music. Gil was a good dancer with a strong lead. And Molly was a good follower, so the fact that they were dancing barefoot on carpet didn't hold them back.

83

As the song continued, *Oh, tell me darling, that you love me...put your little hand in mine...*Gil leaned back and smiled down at her. "Now this is real country music."

Was he mocking her? He'd better not be. Sure it was overly sentimental, cloying even, but she loved it. The old-fashioned melody, the romantic lyrics, the vibrato of the steel guitar that made her heartstrings pulse along with it, all added up to a delicious longing.

"We used to call this kind of song a belly-rubber," Gil said as he pulled her body closer to his.

Stars are smiling, Molly darling...through a misty veil of night... It really is mushy, she thought—and then forgot as their bare feet touched. She could feel the hair of his chest through the gap in his shirt. The base and drum took her along like a slow train.

Do you love me, Molly darling?

He held her close then twirled her around as the last slow words signaled the end of the song. *Let your answer be a kiss.*

He lowered his head and touched his lips to hers as the tremolo of the steel guitar cascaded through her senses. Their bodies pressed together. She felt the heat spread from her pelvis through her solar plexus. She felt her nipples tighten. He kissed her again, thoroughly.

She didn't slap him and she didn't call him a son-of-a-bitch. She stood on her toes and kissed him back with a longing that took her breath away and left her knees weak.

When the kiss ended, the phone was ringing and Eddy Arnold was singing about finding a bluebird. Molly pulled back.

"Don't answer it," Gil said.

"Okay," Molly said.

She stepped back into his arms as the answering machine clicked on. *Hi, this is Molly. Leave a message.* They were kissing again when Jan's voice cut through the moment.

"Hey, Molly. It's Jan. This message is for Gil. I just wanted to confirm our lunch date for tomorrow. Have him give me a call, will you?"

Chapter 23

There was a long moment of suspended animation. Gil's arms still encircled Molly but all movement ground to a halt.

She pushed him away and tried to control her breathing. When she could speak, she said, "You seem to be in great demand with the lonely widows of Missouri."

"Wait, Molly. I did not make a date with that woman. She is assuming—"

Molly flashed on another tall, good-looking man who swore, "I did not have sex with that woman."

"Well, Gil," she said, "Jan obviously thinks otherwise. You'll find her phone number on the caller ID."

"Molly, wait." Gil reached for her. She spun away from him and hit the STOP button on the CD player, cutting Eddie Arnold off in mid-bluebird. The small screen said GOODBYE in digital green letters. *Yes, goodbye . . .*

She left him standing there, running his hand through the silver hair where her fingers had been tangled just moments earlier.

~~

"My God, Liz. I feel like such a fool." She sat at Liz's table ignoring the cup of coffee that had grown cold while she related the events of the previous evening.

"What did he have to say this morning?" Liz asked.

"Nothing. I mean I don't know. I mean I left before he came out of the guestroom."

"So, you stomped off to your room last night, and then left him alone at your house this morning wondering what to do."

"Well, what would you have done?" Molly demanded.

"To start with, I would have grabbed the phone before Jan was through with her message and said, 'I'm sorry, this isn't a good time. Gil and I are just about to have sex.'"

"Yeah, you probably would have," Molly grumbled.

"The point is you didn't give him a chance to explain. Think about it. Jan was all over him at the reception but I didn't hear him agree to meet her for lunch."

"She mentioned lunch as she was leaving and he didn't say anything to contradict her."

"What exactly did she say? Her *exact* words, Molly. Try to remember."

"I don't know. And what difference does it make?"

"It makes a lot of difference when you think about who you're dealing with."

Molly stared into her cold coffee. "The whole thing would probably have been a mistake, anyway. A little too much family connection. Then there's his college education and the uppity way he talks."

"What do you mean, the uppity way he talks?"

"I told you how he described his relationship with his wife— the words he used. Most men would have come right out and said she didn't want to fuck. He just seems a little too high-class for me."

"Bullshit. Nobody's too high-class for you. Look who your best friend is!" Liz declared as she reached inside her blouse and gave her bra strap a tug that raised her left breast to the same level as her right one.

~~

On the way home from Liz's, Molly dreaded the thought of facing Gil. She assumed he would still be at her house, since he wasn't scheduled to fly home until tomorrow. Well, she would be civil, but cool. Maybe he wouldn't even be there. Maybe he'd go home with Jan after their lunch date, stay with her tonight and let her take him to the airport tomorrow.

She thought about her talk with Liz, which caused her to think about how Gil talked. That caused her to think, *Jan's not any damned smarter than I am. She's probably not as smart. I wonder what a conversation between her and Gil would sound like.* A conversation between Jan and Gil. . ..

Molly did a U-turn and sped back to Liz's.

"I remember exactly what Jan said," she shouted when Liz opened the door. "She said, 'Gil, I'll give you a call at Molly's tomorrow. Maybe we can go out to lunch and continue our conversation.' The bitch."

"The bitch," Liz echoed. "And what did Gil say?"

"Nothing. He didn't say anything."

~~

Molly still dreaded the thought of facing Gil, but for a different reason. She would have to apologize, but how to do it without admitting she had reacted like a jealous teenager. *Gil, I'm sorry I flew off the handle. I should have given you a chance to explain.* Wait. She didn't want to sound like she thought he owed her an explanation—even though he had tried to explain.

Okay, how about *I should have ignored the hussy and kept on making out with you.* No. That was wrong on so many levels. How about, *Gil, can we just start over?* No that sounded melodramatic. Start what over? Were they headed for a one-night-stand or something more long-term?

By the time she reached home and opened her front door, Molly still didn't know what she would say to Gil. Maybe he would speak first and set the tone.

It didn't matter. Gil was gone. There was a note on the kitchen table.

Molly,

I changed my flight to today and took a cab to the airport. I hope we can put this behind us and be friends for Richie's and Dennis's sake. Neither one of them would ever forgive me if they thought I'd done something to hurt you.

Two things I want you to know: I don't prey on lonely widows and I didn't make a lunch date with Jan. Well, three things. I'm not sorry I kissed you.

Gil

Molly slumped down in her chair and stared at the note. If it were a movie, or a book, this is where she would jump in her car, race to the airport and try to catch him. She'd get there just before he disappeared through the gate. She'd call his name. He'd turn, rush back and gather her in his arms while the crowd cheered.

Well, it wasn't a movie or a book. It was real life. And if she were honest (and practical) she would see the note as a "whew, that was close" sigh of relief on Gil's part. It was short and sweet and covered everything.

Of course he wanted to be friends for the boys' sake. It wouldn't do to have them find out their horny parents had almost screwed up (pun intended) the family ties just hours after the reception. It made sense he wouldn't want her to think he preyed on lonely widows and it was wise of him to say he didn't have a lunch date with Jan. And of course he would say he wasn't sorry about the kiss, to spare her feelings. He was nothing if not high-class. His handwriting was even neat and precise.

She crumpled the note and threw it in the trash.

Chapter 24

Liz called a couple of hours later. "Can you talk?"

"He's not here, Liz. He was gone when I got home. He left a note. He said he took a cab to the airport."

"Shit. What else did he say?" Liz asked.

"Not much. It was short and sweet."

"Read it to me," Liz demanded.

Molly sighed. "Hold on." She dug the note out of the wastebasket, shook coffee grounds off of it, smoothed it out on the table and read it to Liz. "So that's all there is and there ain't no more," Molly said after she finished reading it. She wadded it up vigorously and threw it back in the trash.

"Hmmm," Liz said. It doesn't exactly sound like the end to me. I think he—"

"Don't even go there, Liz. I'm done with it. I interpret the note as a gentlemanly way of saying, oops, bad move, but let's think about Richie and Dennis and stay on friendly terms—a sort of goofy version of an amicable divorce for the kids' sake."

"What about him saying he wasn't sorry he kissed you?"

"I'm sure that was meant to soothe my ego. Keep me from feeling like such a fool."

"Molly, you're not a fool for getting it on with him, but you're an idiot if you let him get away. You should—"

"Goddammit, Liz," Molly shouted.

"Okay, okay, *okay*. Don't get your bloomers in a bunch. Just let me say one more thing. He's right about Richie and Dennis. You have to let him know you won't show any hard feelings in front of them when he comes to town again. Because he will come to town again."

"I know and I will. I'll send him an email."

89

"When?"

"Soon."

It was like an emotional game of Whack-A- Mole the rest of the day. A thought of THE KISS (Molly had come to think of it in capital letters) would pop up, unbidden, and she would determinedly push it out of her mind. Then a snatch of the THE SONG would pop into her head...*stars are shining, Molly darling*...and THE DANCE would invite itself along. She had to conjure THE BITCH's strident voice...*have him give me a call*...to smack down the memories.

And damn it, those memories were not confined to her head. Her whole body remembered with a thrill that made her knees weak, followed by a jumble of sadness, loss and anger. And confusion. How could the man be under her skin so thoroughly, so soon? She was too practical to believe in love at first sight (or first kiss). Maybe it wasn't about Gil at all. Maybe she just needed to get laid.

~~

Liz called again the next morning. "Did you send it yet?"

"Liz, you need to get a life and stop hounding me."

"I take that to mean no. But that's not the only thing I called about. I'm going to paint the back bedroom and I think you owe me one."

Molly didn't answer.

"Molly, I know you're there. I can hear you breathing. In case you don't remember, I helped you paint that big-assed kitchen of yours and my bedroom is a lot smaller."

"You're right," Molly conceded reluctantly. "When do you want to do it?"

"Now. Joe moved the furniture into the middle of the room last night and covered it with drop cloths. I'll see you in half an hour."

"Pushy bitch," Molly grumbled. "I need to find a better best friend."

"You can't improve on perfection, dear," Liz countered cheerfully. "Now hurry your ass up."

90

Liz handed Molly a paint pan and roller. "Here, you roll and I'll get the edges with a brush." She poured paint into the roller pan then took the can and climbed up on the stepladder.

Molly was unresponsive to Liz's attempts to chat while they worked. She just wanted to get it done and go home.

When she painted as high as she could reach on one wall, she turned to tell Liz she needed the ladder.

She saw Liz had painted FUCK JAN in huge letters near the ceiling and was climbing down from the ladder to admire her handiwork.

Molly regarded the desert sand letters on the sky blue wall. She made her way around the stacked furniture and took the paintbrush out of Liz's hand. She dipped it in the paint can and painted FUCK GIL 2 midway down the wall.

Liz grabbed the stir paddle, dipped it in the paint bucket and drew a stick figure woman with a witch's hat chasing a stick man. She said, "I call it Jan chasing man."

Molly studied it for a moment then took the paddle from Liz and drew a stick man in a stick airplane flying toward three stick mountains. "I call it another man gone." And then the tears came. "Oh, Liz, I miss Sam. I miss him so much."

When Joe got home at 5:30, he found them both sitting on top of the drop cloth that covered the bed, drinking wine coolers. He took in the artistic wall, the pile of empty bottles on the floor and Molly's tear-streaked face.

"I'll go to KFC and get a bucket of chicken," he said.

Chapter 25

When she got home midmorning the next day, Molly went straight to the medicine cabinet, ran a glass of water and washed down two aspirin. Then she lay on her bed and admitted to herself that Joe had been right to take her keys and make her a bed on their living room sofa last night, *"since the guestroom is too fucked up for company."*

Her keys were lying next to the coffee pot this morning. Joe was gone and Liz was still asleep. Molly turned the coffee pot off, let herself out and drove home.

The phone rang at a quarter till noon. Molly rolled over and reached for the extension on the bedside table. She noted with gratitude that she didn't feel a stab of pain in her head when she swung her legs off the bed and sat up.

"Hello."

"Wedding over? Company gone?" It was that deep voice again.

"What do you want?" Molly said.

"I want to get acquainted with you. Have lunch with me."

Molly took a deep breath and let it out slowly. "Not happening. I'm not feeling very kindly toward men in general right now. And you need to stop calling me."

She hung up the phone and went to take a shower.

She got dressed then opened a can of vegetable soup and made toast. The first few bites told her it was going to stay down, so she finished it then had a couple of Hostess Ho Hos and a glass of milk.

Liz called as she was swallowing the last bite.

"Molly, do you feel like shit? I hope so, because misery loves company."

"Sorry to disappoint you, Liz, but I'm beginning to feel human."

"Well, good for you. I feel like a grizzly bear with a burr up its ass. Did you email Gil?"

"I'm going to do it right now. Call me back when you get the burr out of your ass."

It had been two days since Gil left. Molly sat down in front of her computer to compose an answer to his note. It shouldn't be hard. She had cried him out of her system and convinced herself she was *so* over him. She imagined coolness and composure dripping from her fingers into the message as she typed.

Gil,

Sorry it took so long to respond to your note. I've been busy helping Liz with some redecorating. Of course we can put this behind us. No problem. As for Jan, that's entirely between you and her. As for the kiss, it's like it never happened.

Molly

She read it over then deleted the line about Jan. She read it over again and took out the reference to the kiss as well as the excuse about not answering sooner. The final version read:

Gil,

In response to your note, of course we can put this behind us. No problem. It's like it never happened.

Molly

She read it one more time and hit send.

He must have been sitting on top of his computer because she received a reply before she finished checking her other messages.

Like it never happened? Ouch!

She decided to ignore it.

Chapter 26

She went straight from the computer to the guestroom, humming, *Gonna wash that man right outa my hair....* There was a faint trace of Gil's cologne on the sheets she stripped off the bed. She carried them down to the basement and started the washer. The phone rang just as she came back upstairs. The caller ID said H. Holcombe.

She picked up the phone and said, "What?" "This is Hoot."

"I told you to stop calling me."

"Wait, Molly. Don't hang up. Meet me somewhere and have lunch with me before you decide I'm one of those men in general that you're so mad at."

"You've got to be kidding," Molly said. "I don't know you from Adam. Do you really think I'd meet you?"

"Just meet me somewhere public. You name the place. Have lunch with me and I'll come and clean your gutters."

Molly couldn't believe her ears. "You'll do *what?*"

"I'll clean your gutters."

"What makes you think I need my gutters cleaned?" "There's little trees growin' out of them."

"Hold on a minute." She laid the phone down, walked outside and looked up at the guttering. Sure enough, there were twigs sticking up every foot or so. She circled the house with her head tilted back, noting that all the gutters were sprouting debris.

Why hadn't she noticed it and called someone to take care of it? *Because,* she thought bitterly, *that's one of the many things I never had to think about before.* She tried to remember if anyone had cleaned the gutters since Sam died.

She went back inside and picked up the phone. "Are you still there?"

"Yep."

"You know, I'm perfectly capable of getting someone to clean my gutters and do whatever else needs doing around here. I just hadn't noticed. I have a son and his, uhm, his partner. And I could call my son-in-law or I could look in the yellow pages."

"You wouldn't have to if you had a friend like me."

"You don't know anything about me," Molly said, "except that my gutters are full of little trees. What is it that makes you want to be my friend?"

"Just a hunch, Molly. And I never question my hunches."

Molly didn't answer. The silence stretched out until she finally said, "Are you still there?"

"Yep."

"I'll meet you at 54th Street Grill at The Commons Thursday at 1:30." She hung up without waiting for his reply.

I must be out of my freakin' mind.

~~

"He's called you three times and I'm just now hearing about it?" Liz obviously hadn't gotten rid of the burr yet. "Molly, what the hell are you thinking?"

"I don't plan to go alone. That's why I'm calling you." "Jesus, Molly, I think you're rebounding like a rubber ball."

"Tell me what's different about meeting this guy and meeting that Bob the loser from the Senior Matchmaker web site."

"The difference is that was mutual. You were both looking to meet someone. This guy, on the other hand, is taking advantage of a situation. He could be dangerous. Even if he's not dangerous, he must be some kind of a nutcase. That's the damnedest pickup line I ever heard—I'll clean your gutters!"

Molly was quiet while Liz raved on. "What's the guy doing hanging around the HyVee parking lot in the daytime on a weekday? He must not have a job. He's probably a gigolo looking for an innocent widow to—"

"To what, Liz? To change her tire? Clean her gutters? And I'm sure I look innocent but how do you think he knew I was a widow?"

"How do you know he didn't slash your tire?"

"It wasn't slashed. The guy at Mr. Tires said there was a roofing nail in it. Could have picked it up anywhere."

Molly could hear Liz slamming things around in her kitchen. She finally said, "Liz, I'm going, with or without you."

The slamming stopped and she heard Liz blow out a breath. "Fine. But, Molly, if you keep this up, I'm going to have to start carrying a gun."

Molly felt a little shudder at the idea of Liz packing heat.

They agreed to repeat the scenario they had used for Molly's ill-fated meeting with the loser Bob. Liz would follow her to 54th Street Grill, try to get a seat close to them and "get a good look at this character."

Chapter 27

He was leaning against his motorcycle with his arms crossed, worrying a short plastic straw between his teeth. He waited for her to park her car and walk up to him. Today, he wore black jeans, the same black boots with the studded straps and a black denim vest over a white tee shirt.

He took the straw from his mouth and stuck it in a pocket of his vest. "Hey, Molly," he said in that deep, lazy voice. His gaze traveled slowly from her face to her frosted pink toenails inside her strappy aqua sandals, back up the length of her lime green and aqua Capri pants, over her lime green knit top, and settled on her eyes. "You look great," he said. It seemed like an understatement compared to his bold once-over.

She felt herself blush. "Thanks."

He took her arm and they walked into the restaurant. The hostess showed them to a booth near the windows. One of Hoot's legs came in contact with one of hers under the table, sending a quiver of excitement through her body.

The waitress laid menus in front of them and asked what they'd like to drink.

"I'll have iced tea with lemon," Molly said as she saw Liz being led past them.

"Coffee, black," Hoot said.

Liz stopped the hostess who was leading her, spoke to her in a low tone and indicated a booth directly across the room from Molly and Hoot. The hostess shrugged and seated her there.

"You ever ride a motorcycle?" Hoot asked Molly.

"Years ago. My older brother had a big blue Indian. I got on behind him and he took me for a wild ride across a field on my grandparents' farm. He hit a rut, I flew up off the seat and

97

my chin came down hard on his back. I split my lip and bit my tongue. If I hadn't been holding on to him for dear life, I think he would have killed me. He was a crazy, reckless fool with that motorcycle."

"So that left you with a bad attitude toward motorcycles." It was more of a statement than a question.

"Pretty much. I never got on one again."

The waitress came with their drinks and took their orders. Molly asked for a roast turkey sandwich on whole wheat. She was surprised when Hoot ordered a grilled chicken salad with vinegar and oil dressing. She had him figured for a double-bacon-cheeseburger-with-fries kind of guy.

"You told me your aunt and uncle live in my neighborhood," Molly said. "Where, exactly?"

"On Kentucky Road. A little house up on a hill. Name's Holcombe, same as mine. He's my dad's brother."

"Are your parents still living?"

"Nope. How about yours?"

"No."

"Your brother?"

"No. Arnie and Sam—Sam was my husband—both died two years ago."

"I'm sorry," Hoot said. "That must have been tough."

"Tough doesn't begin to—" Molly trailed off as the waitress arrived with their food.

Hoot took a bite of his salad and watched Molly take the top off her sandwich and spread mustard on it. She took another bite and they watched each other chew.

Finally, Hoot said, "I'm not married. I live on the same property where my uncle and aunt are."

Molly just stared at him. "You live with your uncle and aunt? Are you divorced, widowed, or what?"

He smiled. Molly realized it was the first time she had seen him smile. His teeth were very white against his olive complexion. "Never been married. And before you ask, I'm straight. I'll tell you more later. But right now, why don't you ask your friend to join us?" He nodded toward the booth where Liz sat stirring a gob of ketchup with a French fry.

"What friend?" Molly innocently followed his gaze. Liz glanced up, and then looked away quickly. "What makes you think she's a friend of mine?"

"What's her name?"

Molly tried but she couldn't look him in the eye and deny it. She gave a sigh of resignation, slid out of the booth and walked across to Liz. "We're busted. Bring your stuff and come on over."

"What gave us away?"

"I don't know. He just figured it out."

Liz flagged down a waitress and told her she was joining some friends across the room. She picked up her Coke and the waitress brought her burger and fries.

Hoot stood up as they approached. "Hoot Holcombe," he said and offered Liz his hand.

Liz regarded it as if it were a snake for a moment before she took it and said, "I'm Liz." She scooted into the booth beside Molly and glared at Hoot. "So what are you—some kind of psychic Hell's Angel?"

Hoot's gaze didn't falter under Liz's decidedly hostile scrutiny. "Nope, just observant."

Liz's curiosity apparently overcame her hostility and she said, "So tell me. What tipped you off?"

God, first she wants a gun and now she's talking like a chubby little Al Capone, Molly thought. But she was dying to hear the answer, too.

He took another bite of his salad and regarded them thoughtfully while he chewed. Finally, he took a swallow of coffee and said, "First, I didn't expect Molly to come alone. You drove in right behind her but didn't get out of your car until we came inside. Then you got the hostess to seat you where you could see us. The last thing —and I don't know if you'll think this is psychic or not —but there's a bond between you two that's almost tangible."

Molly and Liz looked at each other. Then Liz turned back to Hoot and said, "Damn, you're a spooky sucker!"

Chapter 28

"Well, let's have it," Molly said.

Liz followed her home from 54ᵗʰ Street Grill. She opened the refrigerator, helped herself to a can of Dr. Pepper and sat down opposite Molly.

"I think you've lost your mind, Molly. Sure he's good-looking and he did pick up my lunch tab. But—and there are a lot of buts —I still think he's weird." She paused to take a drink of her soda. "You know he looked through your wallet. He must have found something in there that made him recognize me."

Molly got up, went to her handbag and came back with her wallet. She slid it across the table to Liz. "Do you see a picture of yourself in here? No! Do you see anything else that describes you? Like Molly's best friend: cute as a button, mean as a snake, chubby, sarcastic, stubborn and opinionated?"

"I resent being called chubby," Liz said. She slid the wallet back to Molly without opening it.

"He said he's 58," Liz continued. "That makes him five years younger than you. No offense, but what does a 58-year-old man want with an older woman? Most of them are looking for a sweet young thing.

"And what's with the biker get-up? Seems to me like a case of arrested development. Are you going to buy some geriatric biker boots and go to Sturgis with him and flash your boobs?"

"Gee, Liz. Try not to hold back."

"And another thing, his eyes make me nervous. Every time he looked at me, it felt like an invasion of privacy."

"Yeah, I find that kind of exciting," Molly said.

Just then, Liz, who sat facing the deck, threw her hand over her heart and shrieked, "Oh, my God."

Molly turned around to see what had gotten into Liz. The end of a long aluminum ladder was floating past the windows. They peered through the glass and watched as Hoot propped the ladder against the house.

"Brace yourself," Liz sneered. "You're about to get your gutters violated."

Molly went through to the living room and looked out the triangle of glass in the door. There was a beat-up green truck backed into the driveway. Fading letters on the driver's side door spelled out Big O Lawn Service, Oscar Holcombe Proprietor. There were remnants of a phone number.

Liz came and looked over Molly's shoulder. "This just keeps getting better and better."

For the next half hour, they moved from window to window and watched surreptitiously as Hoot went about his business. Finally, he retracted the telescoping ladder and hung it back on the truck. He got a rake and a brown environmentally approved lawn bag from the truck and began to clean up the debris he had thrown from the gutters.

By the time he worked his way to the back of the house, Molly and Liz were both watching him openly through the glass doors. He seemed to sense their scrutiny. He straightened up, looked directly at them and pulled off his tee shirt. Without breaking his gaze, he used the shirt to wipe sweat off his brow. With his left hand on his hip, he hooked the shirt over his right forefinger, twirled it around a couple of times and tossed it on the ground. He held the pose for a brief moment then resumed his work.

It had been long enough for them to get a load of his chest. And a nice chest it was. A thatch of curly salt and pepper hair covered the broad expanse below his collarbone and tapered to a thin line that ran down his stomach and disappeared under the low waistband of his jeans.

Liz whispered, "Jesus!"

Molly tore herself away from the view and filled three tall glasses with iced tea. She shoved one at Liz, who still had a Dr. Pepper can in one hand, and carried the other two out to the deck.

Alma F. Quick

Hoot wiped his hands on his jeans, picked up his shirt and walked up the steps onto the deck. He accepted the cold glass. "Thanks," he said.

Molly watched him take a long, thirsty drink. "Thought you said your name was Harvey."

"It is."

"So who's Oscar?"

"It's his truck."

"Big O, huh? Very funny."

"My uncle has a bawdy sense of humor. He's entertainin', but harmless."

Molly sipped her tea and studied Hoot. She felt him studying her, too. He seemed totally unselfconscious, sitting on her deck, shirtless and sweaty. She, however, was intensely aware of his bare chest and the musky male scent that emanated from his sweaty body.

"My aunt told me to invite you over Sunday. Come and meet 'em, Molly. I think you'll like 'em."

She heard her phone ring. *Liz'll get it,* she thought, but it kept ringing. After the third ring, she said, "Excuse me." She opened the sliding door and stepped inside. Liz was nowhere in sight. There was a note on the table.

Molly, I'm leaving. I don't think I'll be missed. Call me if you don't get murdered first. Liz.

Oops, she had ignored Liz, but she didn't have to get all snooty about it, did she? While she was shaking her head over the note, the answering machine kicked in.

"Hey, Molly. This is Gil. Please pick up if you're at home." There was a long pause. "Molly, I really want to talk to you. Please call me back. I'm begging your forgiveness."

Molly grabbed the phone off the wall next to the deck door and said, "Hello, Gil. I'm here." She glanced at Hoot, sitting still and serene where she had left him. She wondered if he heard. She slid the door shut, and said, "Sorry, what were you saying, Gil?"

"Oh! Hi, Molly. How are you?"

"I'm good."

102

"Well, umm, Molly, I'm so sorry about the way we left things between us. I'm begging you to give me another chance."

She was distracted, looking at Hoot through the glass. She didn't answer Gil.

"Molly, ever since I met you, and got to know you, I've realized there's been something missing in my life...for years. I know this sounds corny, and I probably shouldn't say it, but I've been thinking about it for days. There's a hole in my life and it's exactly the size and shape of you. Please say you'll give me a chance to get this right."

She watched Hoot stand up. Was he leaving? No, he shook out his tee shirt, fished a piece of plastic straw from the pocket, stuck it between his teeth and sat back down.

Gil was still talking. She interrupted him. "Gil, I'm not mad at you. It's just the way things turned out."

"Ah, Molly, you're breaking my heart. Not mad is the same as indifferent."

Molly was afraid Hoot would leave. She wanted this conversation over with. "I'm sorry, Gil. I don't know what you want me to say. I'll see you when you come to visit the boys again. I can't promise any more than that."

She heard his deep sigh. "Okay, darlin'. I'll have to settle for that."

"Goodbye, Gil." She replaced the phone gently and went back out on the deck. "I'd love to meet your aunt and uncle," she said.

Chapter 29

Liz must have been real worried about me to go off and leave me alone with a potential murderer, Molly thought.

Hoot had left and she knew she should call Liz, but she put it off. For one thing, Liz would probably worm it out of her that she had agreed to go with Hoot to meet his aunt and uncle on Sunday. Molly could hardly believe it herself.

Life's just full of surprises, Molly thought. It wasn't that long ago that she was trolling the Internet, looking for a man. Now she had two of them pursuing her. She walked into the bathroom and looked at herself in the mirror. What had changed?

She went in her office and took her big dictionary off the shelf. *What was that word? Pher, phera, phero...yes, there it is...pheromone–any chemical substance released by an animal that serves to influence the physiology or behavior of other members of the same species.*

She left the dictionary open and went back to the mirror. "Ah, so," she said to her reflection. She bared her teeth and said, "Rowrrr." Good Lord. She covered her face with her hands. She was embarrassing herself.

When Liz answered the phone, Molly said, without preamble, "Liz, I think I've got pheromones."

"You've got what, now? Did you catch it from the biker?"

"No, Liz. Listen to me. Pheromones. I know you've read Erica Jong. She talked about pheromones. Here. I'll read you the definition."

Liz listened while Molly read from the dictionary. As soon as Molly stopped reading, Liz said, "It sounds to me like you're telling me you're in heat."

104

"Be serious for once, Liz. I'm trying to figure out why I'm suddenly so sought after by two men."

"Two men? Who's after you besides the biker dude?"

Oh, crap, I've done it now, Molly thought. There was nothing for it but to tell Liz about the call from Gil.

Liz could hardly contain her excitement. Neither could she contain her disappointment at Molly's lack of it. "Why are you giving him such a hard time, Molly? You were ready to fall into bed with him a few days ago and now he can't catch a break with you."

"I don't know, Liz. When I think about what almost happened, I can't seem to get excited about it."

"Don't tell me you're falling for the gutter-guy."

"Okay, I won't."

"You won't what?"

"I won't tell you I'm falling for him. And his name is Hoot."

"Aw, shit, Molly. You're going to be riding around Independence on the back of a Harley while Jan cruises the world with Gil. What the hell is wrong with you?" Her voice rose several decibels on the question.

"As long as you're already all worked up, you might as well know I'm going to meet his aunt and uncle on Sunday," Molly said, and waited for the explosion. But Liz was silent.

"Liz?"

"Yeah?"

"Say something."

"Something. Call me when you get home. If you get home," she added, darkly, and hung up.

Chapter 30

Molly folded laundry the next morning when the phone rang just before noon. She glanced at the caller ID and saw the call was coming from a pay phone. Oh, damn, it was probably Charlie again. Maybe she needed to tone down the pheromones a little.

"Hey, Molly. How ya doin', girl?"

"I'm okay, Charlie. Why are you calling from a pay phone?"

"I'm up here on 24 getting some gas and I thought I'd call and see if you're better. You were feeling a little puny the last time I talked to you. Anyhoo, what are you doing right this minute?"

"I'm doing laundry."

"Hey, I'm practically right around the corner. How's about I pick you up in 10 minutes and we can run out to Denny's and grab some lunch."

"Charlie, I'm not dressed to go anywhere."

"You don't need to be dressed to go to Denny's. Well, omygosh, I mean you need to be dressed but you don't need to be dressed up."

"But, I'm on a diet."

That sounded lame, even to her.

"That's okay," he said. "You can just get a salad. I'll see you in a few."

"Charlie? Wait!" But she was talking to a dial tone.

Molly was plenty steamed by the time Charlie rang the bell. She opened the door. Before he could get a word out, she said, "Charlie Hickman, I'm not going to Denny's or anywhere else. It's too bad you didn't let me tell you that before you hung up. You could have saved yourself the trip."

106

Charlie hung his head. "Omygosh, I messed up didn't I? I'm sorry, Molly. Don't be mad. I'd rather poke an eye out than have you mad at me."

What a pitiful figure. Molly felt her anger begin to ebb. "Oh, for crying out loud, Charlie, I'm not mad. But I'm still not going anywhere. Look at me." She was wearing a pair of faded denim crop pants, an old shirt of Sam's that was way too big for her, and a pair of fluorescent green flip-flops. "And I *am* on a diet. I was just getting ready to make myself a salad."

Charlie stuck his hands in his pockets and sighed. "I'm sorry, Molly. Anyhoo, let me just say this, then I'll get out of your hair. You look beautiful to me no matter what you're wearing. And I don't see why you need to be on a diet at all."

Molly thought, *Aw, shit.* She said, "Okay, here's an idea. I'm not leaving the house looking like this, but if you're interested in a sandwich, you can join me for lunch here."

Charlie's demeanor couldn't have changed any faster. Molly thought that if he were a puppy he would have wagged his tail and yipped at her heels all the way to the kitchen.

She poured prewashed salad mix into two bowls, set out a couple of bottles of dressing and made a fresh pot of coffee. She set a loaf of whole wheat bread, a package of deli turkey meat and a couple of individually wrapped slices of fat free cheese on the table and told him to help himself. After a short internal debate, charity prevailed and she put half a dozen chocolate chip cookies on a small plate and set them in front of him along with a tall glass of milk.

She sat at the table with her salad and watched Charlie build himself two sandwiches.

"Charlie," she said, "you keep calling me from pay phones. Don't you have a phone at home?"

"Well...umm...say, do you watch Letterman?" Without waiting for her to answer, he went on to talk about a regular segment called *Great Moments in Presidential Speeches*, that showed clips of President Bush saying things that made him sound particularly stupid.

Molly said she had seen several of them and remarked that they certainly had a wealth of material to draw from.

Charlie segued from *The Late Show* into a rant about local politicians. He held forth on their virtues and corruptions while he worked his way through two sandwiches, the bowl of salad, and four of the cookies.

When there were two cookies left, he offered the plate to Molly. She shook her head and he finished them off. Then he drained the last of his milk, leaned back in his chair, stretched his gangly legs out under the table and crossed his hands over what would have been his belly if he had one.

He smiled at her, a smile of utter contentment. "Molly, girl," he said, "you sure know how to take care of a man."

She thought, *Oh, shit!*

Charlie's gaze wandered around the kitchen in a leisurely inventory, then settled on the patio doors that led to her deck and generous back yard beyond. "This is quite a place you've got here, girl. Quite a place."

When Molly didn't answer, he went on in a trance-like voice.

"But ya know what I'd do with this place? I'd sell it and move to the country. Get me some land and put my trailer on it. Maybe build a little house later. Have me a couple of horses. You like horses, hon?"

Holy shit! Molly stood up and stepped back from the table. She noted with alarm that Charlie was between her and the wall phone. But then she looked at him, sitting there all smug and content with a belly full of her food, plotting how to spend the proceeds from the sale of her house, and her alarm turned to cold anger.

"Charlie, I hate to rush you but you need to leave now. My son will be here any minute to help me move some boxes," she lied.

He came out of his reverie, slowly reeled his legs in and stood up. "Oh, well, omygosh, okay. I hope I didn't say something wrong."

He kept talking as she herded him from the kitchen, through the living room and out the front door. "Well, thanks for lunch, I really enjoyed it, and golly gee, I'm sorry I didn't give you more notice."

She stood in the doorway and watched him leave. He turned, halfway down the walk, and said, "Okay then, I'll call you."

"Don't." She said it quietly but firmly.

He clutched his heart in a dramatic gesture, as if he'd been stabbed. "Really? Aw, Molly, girl. Golly gee. Are you saying you never want to hear from me again? Omygosh, what did I do?"

Molly shook her head and closed and locked the door. She continued to watch him through the triangle of glass until he shrugged and turned away. Perhaps he sensed that his plans for the future had taken a bad turn. He got in his red Escort wagon and drove away.

Molly punched number four on her speed dial.

Liz answered with her usual terse, "Yeah?"

"Liz, it's me. I need to ask you a question."

"It's your dime. Shoot."

"When I told you about my date with Charlie, what was it that made you say I needed to get rid of him?"

"Oh, God, Molly. Don't tell me you're thinking about going out with him again."

"Not in this lifetime. But I want to know what you picked up on that I missed." She proceeded to tell Liz about Charlie's surprise visit.

After Molly finished relating her story, Liz said, "Okay, Grasshopper. Pretend you're sitting at my feet. Listen and learn.

"No offense, Molly, but if it had been dumpy old me, newly widowed, that he ran into at the funeral, he would have given me the same kind of rush he gave you.

"Then there was the letter and the disclosure about his financial situation. He was already planning a merger before the first date. And he's a cheapskate. He wanted to impress you by taking you to a halfway decent place for dinner, but he might as well have come right out and told you he didn't want to pay for a drink or a steak."

"But, Liz, I thought he— "

"Ah, ah, ah. Let me finish. Now here's where you and I are different. If he had pulled that 'I'm having iced tea and chicken' crap on me, I would have ordered something from the bar and the most expensive steak on the menu. I might've had to ask for a separate check and haul out my credit card. But I would've shone a light on his true colors, right then and there."

"Anything else, Master?"

"As a matter of fact, yes. The car. It doesn't bother me what kind of car he drives or what it looks like if it runs. But he could have cleaned out the trash before he picked you up. Honey, he's a slob. And there's just one more thing. Why doesn't he have a phone?"

"How do you know he doesn't?"

"Elemental, my dear. He communicates by pay phone and the U.S. mail."

"So, Liz, why didn't I see what you saw? When you lay it out, it's all pretty clear, but it went right over my head."

"Number one, you're vulnerable and that makes you an easy target. And number two, you're just too damn nice. Opportunists are attracted to vulnerability like rats to cheese. Remember how your dad used to say that if there was a loser or a con man in the crowd, he'd sniff the air and head straight for you?"

Molly remembered. But she had thought the curse was lifted when she met Sam.

Chapter 31

Hoot came to the door at 11:15 on Sunday morning with a black helmet on his head and a blue one tucked under his arm. He handed the extra one to her. "Blue, to match your eyes," he said.

Molly wondered if he had bought it just for her. She put the helmet on her head. Hoot stepped closer, adjusted the helmet, fastened the strap and tested the tension.

He took her hand and they walked down the steps to the driveway. Molly eyed the Harley. Fear sucked all the saliva from her mouth.

Hoot squeezed her hand. "Don't be nervous. I'll be gentle." The way he said it made her almost as nervous as the idea of getting on the bike.

Hoot mounted the Harley in his usual loose, graceful style and patted the seat behind him. Molly hesitated. She was too short to throw her leg over like he did. What was she supposed to hold on to? If it were a horse, at least she'd have some stirrups and a saddle horn.

After a moment, Hoot dismounted, picked Molly up and set her on the bike. Then he got back on, reached behind him with both hands and pulled her up against him. "Just snuggle up tight and wrap your arms around me."

The motor roared to life, sending vibrations through her body. She tightened her arms around Hoot as the bike began to roll. It didn't take long to get the feel of Hoot leaning into the turns. She was soon relaxing into the turns with him, although she did not loosen her arms. She was intensely aware of the contact with his body—from her pelvis against his hips to her breasts against his back. She already knew the ride would end too soon.

The thought had barely crossed her mind when the bike slowed and turned onto a gravel lane that sloped steeply up the hill. Hoot guided the bike expertly up to the front porch of the small house.

A tall man and a very small woman stood on the porch smiling. The man rushed down the porch steps and plucked Molly off the bike. He set her on the ground and grinned down at her. "You sure are a pretty little thing." His deep, slow drawl sounded very much like Hoot's.

The tiny woman hurried down the steps and scolded, "Oscar, you can back off now. You'll be scarin' the poor girl to death."

Hoot slid off the bike, picked the little woman up and swung her around. She pounded him on the shoulders and squealed, "Put me down! What is it with you Holcombe men?" But she was smiling.

Hoot set her down gently and turned to Molly. "Molly, this is my Aunt Emily and Uncle Oscar. I call 'em Little Em and Big O." Emily beamed at Hoot as if he had said something incredibly brilliant.

"I'm happy to meet you," Molly said. She offered her hand to Emily, who ignored it and moved in to hug her instead. Then she took Molly by the arm and guided her toward the house. Molly was relieved she didn't have to decide whether or not Oscar would settle for a handshake.

Molly paused on the porch to take the helmet off. She handed it to Hoot and blessed her naturally curly hair as she ran her fingers through it and fluffed it out.

Emily, whose frizzy white angel hair seemed to be trying to escape from her head, watched admiringly. "My, weren't you in the right line when they passed out hair!" she said.

Inside, Emily bustled about, making everyone comfortable, offering drinks. She refused Molly's offer to help. She assured them lunch would be ready soon, and disappeared into the kitchen, from which delicious smells emanated.

"She's makin' one of her mysterious stews," Oscar confided. Then, as if they had rehearsed the act, Oscar and Hoot yelled, in perfect unison, "Hey, Little Em, need some help?"

Emily stuck her head around the door and shook a large spoon in their direction. "You two just keep your big, clumsy selves out of my kitchen."

Within 15 minutes, the dining room table was laid with a meal fit for a dozen farmhands. There was a steaming pot of stew, a mound of fluffy mashed potatoes and plate of perfectly browned fat biscuits. A platter of bright red sliced tomatoes added color to the array. Molly watched, fascinated, as Oscar scooped a spoonful of the mashed potatoes onto his plate and covered them with stew. *How strange*, she thought, *but when in Rome....* She dipped mashed potatoes onto her plate and covered them with stew. One bite told her Oscar was onto something.

Hoot and Oscar heaped lavish praise on Emily's culinary skills.

Molly agreed. She said, "Emily, this is the kind of meal I remember my grandma laying out for a bunch of neighbors when they came to help my grandpa put up hay. They called the noon meal dinner instead of lunch and there was a huge bell mounted on a tall pole with a rope hanging down. Grandma rang it to call them in from the field."

Emily and Oscar exchanged a look. Oscar nodded and turned to Hoot. "Wouldya listen to that, son. She talks like a farm girl."

Molly blushed, but it sounded like a compliment.

She was debating how obvious it would be to sneak open the button on her jeans when Emily made another foray into the kitchen and emerged with four dishes of berry cobbler, each topped with a generous scoop of ice cream.

"Oh, my God, I've died and gone to heaven," Molly murmured.

As Emily set Oscar's dessert in front of him, he patted her tiny bottom with his big hand and said, "She's little, but she's mighty, ain't she?"

"Stop that, Oscar. Behave yourself," Emily hissed.

113

Molly would have bet Emily's blush was more about pleasure than embarrassment.

Hoot grinned at their antics and winked at Molly.

When Emily seemed satisfied that nobody could possibly hold another bite, she got up and started to clear the table. Molly rose and began to help, halfway expecting to be told to stay out of Emily's kitchen. But that didn't happen and they worked in companionable cooperation.

Emily's hands were in sudsy dishwater nearly up to her elbows when Oscar stuck his head in the kitchen and said, "Ladies, me and Hoot are gonna walk over to the roost. Come on over when you're through."

"Take that plate of leftovers out to the dog on your way," Emily said.

"What's the roost?" Molly asked.

Emily lifted her right hand out of the water, shook suds off it and pulled back the curtains over the sink. "That's it, right over there."

Molly peeked over Emily's shoulder. There was a grand house with the same white siding and gray trim as the house they were in. It sat to the back and west of Oscar and Emily's house, nestled among a grove of big trees.

"Who lives there?"

"Hoot."

"That's Hoot's house?"

"Yep, Hoot's Roost. He tried to get me and Oscar to move in, but we're happy right here."

"But, why, I mean—" Molly stammered, thinking that the house she and Emily stood in would fit inside the roost with a lot of room to spare.

Emily turned from the window and watched Molly for a moment. "Honey, you're about to rub the pattern off that plate." She gently took the plate from Molly's hand. "How long have you known Hoot?"

"Not long."

"Harrumph. Men!" Emily let the water out of the sink, and dried her hands. She sat down at the small table in the

114

kitchen and motioned for Molly to sit. "Tell me what you know about him."

Molly took a deep breath and told Emily how she had met Hoot. She ended by saying, "And my best friend, Liz, is worried that he's a gigolo, looking for a lonely widow to bilk out of her savings because he doesn't seem to be gainfully employed."

"And what do you think?" Emily asked.

"I haven't made up my mind," she shrugged.

"And yet, you got on his motorcycle and rode to a stranger's house with him."

Molly looked into Emily's eyes for a hint as to whether she was being chastised. But she saw only amusement.

"He's a charmer, ain't he? Takes it after his Uncle Oscar, I reckon." Em slapped her thigh and laughed.

Chapter 32

"Let's walk over there," Emily said.

They found Oscar and Hoot sitting in a couple of bright yellow Adirondack chairs on a sunny deck that spanned the entire back of Hoot's house and looked out on a wooded area.

Hoot jumped up. "Sit down. Join us."

"No, no." Emily said. "I just came to drag Oscar back to our house. I know it's Sunday, but I've got a honey-do list for him."

Oscar stood. Molly thanked both of them for their hospitality and complimented Emily again on her wonderful cooking.

They assured Molly she was welcome to come again any time and told her they had enjoyed meeting her. Then Oscar took Emily's hand and they walked back to the little house.

Molly smiled, watching them swing their clasped hands between them like a couple of teenagers. She had an inappropriate thought about Emily's honey-do list.

Hoot arranged the chairs so they were facing each other and motioned for Molly to sit. He opened a cooler beside his chair and took out two ice-cold beers. He twisted off the caps and handed one to Molly.

"What do you want to know?" he said. He leaned forward, his arms resting on his thighs, the beer bottle dangling in his right hand.

Molly took sip of beer. "Tell me about Harvey Hoot Holcombe."

Hoot sat back in his chair and gazed at the woods with a faraway expression. "I'm an only child. I would've been an orphan if Little Em and Big O hadn't taken me to raise after my mom and dad died."

"What happened to them?" Molly asked.

"A car wreck. They were both killed instantly."

"Where were you when it happened?" Molly asked gently.

"They'd left me with Em and O. They were celebratin' their anniversary." He drank some more beer.

"My God," Molly whispered. How awful for you." She lifted her bottle and drank when he continued.

"I don't really remember any of it. I was only 3 years old. I'm just tellin' the story the way it's been told to me."

"So Emily and Oscar raised you as their own?"

"Oh, yeah. And it's been such a good life with them, sometimes I think I wouldn't have wanted it any other way. Then, of course, I feel guilty for thinkin' that. But I still do. Think that, I mean. Em and O couldn't have kids of their own and they raised me just like I was theirs. I couldn't have asked for a better life."

"They seem like wonderful people, Molly said, "I'm surprised you don't call them Mom and Dad."

Hoot fished a ragged piece of plastic straw out of his vest pocket and stuck it in his mouth. After a moment, he said, "That was Em's idea. She wanted me to remember my parents and thought if I called her and Big O Mom and Dad, I would forget about my real ones. Besides, they were already Aunt Em and Uncle O to me."

"Which one is your blood relative" Molly asked.

Hoot chuckled. "Both."

"Both?"

"Yep. My mom and Em were sisters and my dad and Oscar were brothers. Em and my mom are one half Indian. Their dad was full-blooded Seneca Iroquois. Em knows a lot of nature stuff and she taught me what she knows. I could take you into the woods, build a shelter, start a fire and provide food."

"Wow," Molly said. "When I walk in the woods I prefer it to be on a nature path. And it's a good walk if I never see a spider."

Hoot smiled and shook his head. "Spiders have their good points."

"Like hell," Molly said with a shudder. "What about your dad and Oscar? Do they have Indian blood?"

"My dad and Big O were Ozark hillbillies. I don't know if they civilized their wives or vice versa. So what else would you like to know?"

"Tell me about these two houses."

"My dad and Big O bought this land when they came to the city. They each built a small house. Em and O still live in the one Big O built. When I was 21, they turned the one my dad built over to me. I've been tinkerin' with it ever since."

"Tinkering? You mean you turned a little house like Oscar's and Emily's into this—this—"

Hoot stood up, walked to the other end of the deck and tossed the piece of plastic straw over the rail. He stood with his back to Molly for several minutes. When he returned to his chair, he said, "I started out with what I thought was a noble intention of enlargin' it and tradin' with Em and O. But Em wouldn't hear of it. She said Oscar carried her across the threshold of her little house and that's where she'll live until she dies."

"Didn't you ever get married?"

"Nope. Got my heart broke when I was real young."

She waited. "I guess you're not going to talk about that?"

"Not yet." The lines in Hoot's face seemed to deepen. He finished his beer and set the bottle down.

Molly wanted to know a lot more, but she sensed the subject was closed. She said, "Hoot, you're obviously not an unemployed bum like Liz believes. What do you do for a living?"

"I'm a geek."

Molly raised an eyebrow and waited.

"A computer geek. 'Course, it sounds better when I say computer consultant. I fix computer problems, for companies and individuals. I do beta testing on new software. Advise my clients on whether their current systems will work with new software. That kind of stuff. Sometimes I'm really busy and sometimes I don't have much work." He smiled and added, "So you can tell Liz I'm an honest, *sometimes* hard-workin' citizen."

"How did you get into computers?" Molly asked.

"Before I turned Geek, I worked on the assembly line at the Ford plant. One day I just decided I'd had enough. I knew I'd do better workin' for myself. So I went to DeVry and studied Geek. I don't think I fit into society real well."

"Why do you think that?" Molly asked. "You're intelligent, quite presentable and you have a sense of humor."

"Let me give you an example," Hoot said. There was this gal I worked with at Ford. I thought we were pretty good friends and I brought her home to meet Little Em and Big O. We were all standin' around gettin' acquainted when that worthless hound, Duke, sauntered up and laid down at Big O's feet. Well, old Duke had a bad flatulence problem. When he started to pass gas, Big O gave him a nudge with his toe and yelled, 'Git outa here, you mangy hound.' Then he turned to my friend and said, 'I know that sorry mutt couldn't of et anything that smells that bad. Somethin' musta crawled up his ass and died.'"

Molly laughed until tears ran down her face.

"Now see," Hoot said. "You thought that was funny. I thought it was funny and I laughed. Well, she didn't laugh. Her eyes darted around like a caged animal and she told me to take her home. She avoided me at work after that."

Molly dug a tissue from her pocket and wiped her eyes. Then she finished her beer and handed the empty bottle to Hoot. "So besides my raunchy sense of humor, what else attracts you to me, Hoot?"

"It started the first time I saw you, with the way you handled produce in HyVee."

Molly couldn't imagine where he was going with that thought. "What are you talking about?"

"The way you picked up a cantaloupe, pressed both ends and smelled it. Then there was the cucumber."

"What?" Molly wasn't sure she wanted to hear any more.

"The cucumber," Hoot repeated. "You picked it up, squeezed it and sort of caressed it, and then you laid it down, patted it and walked away with a dreamy smile on your face."

"I did not!"

"Yes you did. And then when I heard you cuss like a sailor over your flat tire, I was hooked. I knew you were an earthy, excitin' woman. Besides all that, I liked your looks.

"Come on." Hoot stood and pulled Molly to her feet. "I'll show you the inside of the roost."

Chapter 33

Hoot slid the patio door open. As she started to move past him, he scooped her up in his arms and carried her through the door.

"What are you doing?" she demanded.

"Sorry," Hoot said. "Somethin' just came over me." He let her slide slowly to the floor, keeping his right arm in contact with her body.

Molly moved away from him and looked around. They were in a big, airy kitchen. Gleaming stainless steel appliances were built into solid beech cabinets with beautiful black granite countertops. A spacious island in the center, with two stools tucked under one end, had a fantastic array of storage options. The windows above the sink looked out onto the deck and the wooded area beyond. It was a kitchen any woman would die for.

"So, when Emily turned down your offer to trade houses, you turned this one into a real showplace to live in by yourself?" Molly asked. "Are you sure you're not—" She let the words trail off.

Hoot looked at her. "What? Gay? Nope. You want me to prove it?"

She felt her face flush and changed the subject. "And you live here by yourself?"

Yep. I've kinda made the house into a hobby. It started out a lot smaller and I just kept buildin' on. Got everything in this room on sale from a display kitchen."

"That's what Richie and Dennis do sometimes," Molly said. "My son and his partner. They buy display rooms for their remodels. They buy run-down houses, fix them up and re-sell them."

Hoot led her out of the kitchen into a hallway and opened another door that revealed a large room full of computer equipment. "This is where I work."

There were two computer stations and a long table covered with an array of computers in various stages of repair, surrounded by a tangle of cables and wires. What looked to be the main workstation was situated in front of a row of floor-to-ceiling windows. One wall held a built-in book- case filled with technical manuals. An entire shelf was taken up with a row of jewel cases inserted at a slant to allow easy reading of their labels.

"My, God," Molly whispered. How do you keep track of everything? That table," she nodded toward the work area, "looks like a den of snakes."

"It's a lot more organized than it looks. I know who every piece belongs to and I'll either cure 'em or deliver the bad news after the diagnosis."

"I would have guessed almost anything but computer consultant," Molly murmured. "Wait 'til I tell Liz."

"Will she be surprised or disappointed when you tell her you found computer parts instead of body parts?" Hoot turned the full force of those unfathomable eyes on her.

"Come on," he said. I'll show you my favorite room in the house."

Molly fully expected to be shown a bedroom. But he led her back into the hall and opened the next door.

The room it revealed was slightly larger than the one they had just left. It had the same floor-to-ceiling window arrangement. The centerpiece of the room was a rather battered piano. An oak bar with four padded stools occupied about half of the inside wall. A mirror behind the bar reflected an assortment of bottles and glasses. There was a small round oak table and four straight-back chairs in the floor space between the bar and the windows on the outside wall. The only art on the walls was a 12x14 frame near the bar, which held a collage of snapshots.

Molly studied the photos. The one she found most intriguing showed a younger Hoot sitting on a bench in front of a piano, which had a huge red bow on top of it. He was surrounded by a group of people. On his left were a petite blond woman, and a paunchy grey-haired man with a proprietary arm around the woman's waist. On Hoot's right, a skinny man with a white beard and bushy eyebrows raised a bottle of beer in an apparent toast to Hoot. Everyone had big smiles on their faces except for Hoot, who simply looked dazed.

She looked from the snapshot to Hoot and back again. She said, "It's your piano."

"From that day on it was," he said. He flopped down on the piano bench and ran his fingers idly over the keys then began to play. Molly recognized the melody, "Getting to Know You". She moved to the end of the piano and watched him. He segued into an Elvis song, "It's Now or Never."

He grinned at her and raised an eyebrow. She smiled and shook her head, ever so slightly. Hoot shrugged and began to play a medley of gospel music, all of which Molly recognized from her enforced church attendance as a child. Hoot's rendering of these "church songs" sounded like a cross between honky-tonk and gospel. In spite of the jazzed up versions, she identified "In the Garden", "Precious Memories" and "Amazing Grace".

Hoot stopped playing and let his arms fall to his sides, Molly said, "I'm surprised. You don't seem like the type who would play gospel music."

"And I'm surprised," Hoot said. "You don't seem like the type who would recognize it." He stood and regarded Molly with a long, intense gaze. "Can you name the tunes?" he asked.

Molly easily named them, in order, ticking them off on her fingers. "Pretty good," Hoot said. "Do you play?"

Why does everything he says seem to have a double meaning? She said, "No, I don't play. I just appreciate."

"Nothin' wrong with that. Players need appreciation. I love it when the congregation shows their appreciation."

Molly broke eye contact with an effort and walked back to the collage of snapshots. He didn't say audience, he said congregation. And yet, this room appeared to be a replica of

123

a neighborhood beer joint. She shook her head. "Congregation? You make it sound like a church thing."

"It is," Hoot said, walking up behind her. "I play the last Sunday of every month at Unity over on 39th."

"I don't think I believe you," Molly said. She turned around. Hoot was so close she could feel his breath.

"Come and see for yourself." He looked into her eyes. "There's a lot you don't know about me, Molly." After a pause, he continued, "Maybe a lot you don't want to know. For example, right now I'm tryin' hard to keep my hands off of you."

I must like living dangerously, Molly thought, as she stood her ground. "Why?" She said and waited to see what would happen next.

And it wasn't what she expected. Hoot reached out and touched her face, a feather-light touch. He ran his thumb slowly over her lips. His eyes never left hers.

Molly trembled, ready to succumb to whatever he had in mind.

Suddenly, he dropped his hand from her face, turned with a groan and walked away.

Molly watched him close the piano lid and move toward the door. "Hoot," she said loudly, "what the bloody hell was that all about? I'll be damned if I understand you. What do you want from me? Do you enjoy messing with me?"

He turned around and walked back to her. "There you go, cussin' like a sailor again. Do you know it turns me on to hear that kinda talk comin' out of your pretty mouth? I'd love to hear you really talk dirty. And I'd love to mess with you." He shook his head. "Not really. Come on. I'm takin' you home."

"Now?" Molly asked. Her knees felt wobbly.

"Yes, now." He touched her face again, tenderly. "I know you don't trust me. You've got a lot of questions in your mind about me. And yet you're thinkin' you'd like to live dangerously and have a little fling with me."

Molly stared at him. How did he know what she was thinking?

"I'd like that, too," he continued. "But when I make love to you," his voice was deep and gruff as he said, "and someday

124

I'm gonna make love to you, I want you to give me everything you've got—and take everything I've got and keep comin' back for more. Not have your little adventure and then go back to your safe life and forget about me."

"Hoot," Molly's voice was barely above a whisper, "I...I...I have to pee before we get back on the bike."

"God, you're so romantic. It's at the end of the hall. I'll wait for you on the deck."

Chapter 34

Molly paced. It had been five days since Hoot abruptly ended her visit and brought her home.

She hadn't seen or heard from him. She went over every detail in her mind, again and again. My, God, she had been so aroused she would have allowed him to take her right then, on the floor. But, she chastised herself, she had also been ready to fall into bed with Gil not long before. Maybe she was just horny.

She stopped pacing and sat down, her head in her hands. She tried to recall every detail of her almost moment, as she had come to think of it, with Gil. She had been aroused then, too. She tried to picture Gil's eyes. They were...green? Gray? No, blue. *Definitely blue.* She thought.

Her mind wandered unbidden, to Hoot's eyes. She had no trouble picturing them. They were deep, dark pools that seemed to grow darker the longer he gazed into hers. They probed her soul. Stop! Back to Gil's eyes.

The ringing phone pierced her meanderings. She let the answering machine get it.

"Molly, goddamnit, if you don't pick up, I'm going to set your house on fire and smoke you out!" Liz shrieked. "I know you're there. Now. PICK. UP."

Molly sighed, lifted the receiver and turned off the recorder in the middle of Liz's tirade. "Jesus, Liz, you're supposed to be my best friend, not my drill sergeant. What the hell do you want?"

"I'll be at your door in 10 minutes. I want you to let me in and talk to me. That's what the hell I want. And I wouldn't mind a beer and some chips, too."

~~

Liz regarded the two bottles of Bud Light making sweat rings on the unadorned table and the unopened bag of Sun chips. "You really shouldn't have gone to so much trouble," she said as she stomped to the cupboard, got a bowl, opened the bag of chips and poured them into the bowl. She brought two placemats to the table, picked up the bottles and placed them on the mats. Only then did she sit down and begin the inquisition.

"Okay, you've been avoiding me. You didn't even call when you got home from your tryst with the biker."

"He has a name. His name is Hoot."

"I don't care what his name is. You've had me worried to death. I want details and I want them now."

Molly took a long swallow of beer and slammed the bottle down. "Okay, here it is: His aunt and uncle are lovely people. They live in a small house on a hill. Hoot lives in a big house on the same hill. He's a computer geek. He works from home. He's one quarter Indian. He plays the piano like an angel. He plays everything from country to gospel. Even plays at church once a month. He's got sexy he hasn't tapped into yet. And just about the time I was ready to let him have his way with me, he left me panting with lust, made it clear he wanted more than a one-night stand, and brought me home. I haven't heard from him since. Oh, Liz, I'm so confused."

"Well, put on your big girl pants and get ready to deal with it," Liz said around a mouthful of chips. She washed them down with a several swigs of beer. "Things are about to get worse. Gil's coming to town in a couple of weeks and wants to see you. He called and begged me to plead his case. And before you ask, I don't know how he got my number. Maybe he asked your son, or his. It sounds like you swallowed everything the biker told you, hook, line and sinker," she said, switching subjects so fast Molly didn't have a chance to ask about Gil.

"For your information, Liz, most of it is indisputable fact. I met the aunt and uncle and formed my own opinion. I was in both houses on the hill, I saw the computers Hoot works on, I heard him play the piano and I can tell you he's sexy as hell. The only thing I can't confirm is that he plays the piano in church. Now let's have the news about Gil's visit. I'm not ready for this, but lay it on me anyway."

"Don't sound so put-upon. A lot of women would love to have your problems.

"Here's what Gil is planning. He wants to get the boys to have a big housewarming party. Figures it's something you wouldn't dare blow off—and something he would be expected to attend. Richie and Dennis were less than enthusiastic about it from what Gil says. But he's not giving up."

"Just like a man," Molly said. "Does he think he can come here in two weeks and suddenly make a party materialize — even if he talks the boys into it? What about invitations and refreshments and decorations and so forth?"

Liz leaned over the table and brushed S u n chip crumbs off her bosom. "The invitations would be a problem. The rest of it, Richie and Dennis could handle without breaking a sweat, I'm fairy sure. I mean fairly. *Fairly* sure."

Molly threw her placemat at Liz.

~~

After Liz left, Molly promptly put Gil's impending visit out of her mind and resumed her ruminations about Hoot. She pulled the magnetized calendar off the refrigerator and laid it on the table in front of her. How long should she wait for him to call? And what difference did it make? What would she do about it if he didn't call in the next few days...or weeks...or ever? As she gazed at the calendar, it occurred to her that this coming Sunday was the last Sunday of the month. Hmmm.

She retrieved last Saturday's newspaper from the recycle stack in the garage. Several Unity churches were listed in the Faith section, but none on 39ᵗʰ Street. She leaned back in her chair and tried to come to terms with the idea that he'd lied about playing at church. Her disappointment was visceral. She felt nauseated. *Oh well, that's what I get for being so quick to fall in...what? Love, like, heat...or whatever I've fallen in.*

As she sat staring at the newspaper, her eye fell on .com at the end of another Unity church's listing. She felt a ridiculous rush of hope. You're pathetic, she told herself as she headed for her computer.

Chapter 35

The church was small compared to other churches on 39th and was set back farther from the street. The website had said Sunday service started at 10 a.m. The clock on her dash said 9:56. Molly found a parking space toward the back of the gravel lot. She heard music coming from the building, piano music. She looked around. There were a lot of cars. And there were half a dozen motorcycles parked on a grassy area beyond the gravel lot. *Good grief, what kind of a church is this?*

She sat behind the wheel, immobilized. What should she do? Just walk in? Would people turn around and look at her? She hadn't been inside a church in years. And she couldn't remember ever walking into a church alone. The clock on her dash now said 10 on the dot. *Too late,* she told herself. The service had already started. She was on the verge of driving away when another car zoomed into the lot, screeched to a halt next to her and disgorged two couples. They headed for the building, seemingly unconcerned about being late.

Molly got out of her car, squared her shoulders and followed them. The two couples entered ahead of her and seated themselves.

Molly, however, stood rooted to the spot, her eyes on Hoot. Yes, he was playing a piano at one end of the platform. And he was singing. It was the first time she had heard him sing. She couldn't identify the song—something about being free and unlimited.

It occurred to her that she was still standing. She moved to an empty seat at the far end of the back row. At that moment, Hoot looked up and she knew he saw her. He trailed off the song he was playing and ran a riff on the keyboard that became *Hello darlin, it's nice to see you,* which he talked more than sang in true Conway Twitty fashion. Molly felt her face burn as she sank into the seat.

But Hoot wasn't through. He ran another little riff and hummed four notes and then softly sang the two words, *Molly, darling.*

The minister, a woman dressed in a flowing purple garment, turned from the podium and looked at Hoot. He flashed her a brilliant smile and began what Molly could only describe as a holy romp of some sort on the piano. He sang *I've got the power of love in my soul.* As he sang and pounded out the music on the piano, the entire congregation came to their feet. They clapped and swayed and sang along. Molly had never seen anything like it in church. She found herself standing and clapping along with the others, though she didn't know the words.

When the song ended, the congregation applauded and whooped like what you would expect in a honky-tonk bar. Well it had kind of sounded like honky-tonk, the way Hoot played it.

When the applause died down, the minister said, "Aren't we blessed to have Harvey Holcombe with us this morning? Sometimes he's full of surprises, but we're always blessed." That set off another round of applause.

Hoot turned to the minister and did a little bow thing. With his hands in prayer position, he dipped his head toward her. Then he turned to the congregation and repeated the motion. Molly had seen Oprah do the same thing on TV. She supposed it was some sort of acknowledgment, which meant *thank you* or *bless you* or something.

"And now," the minister said, "it's time to greet your neighbors. We're a friendly bunch here, so if you don't want a hug, get your hand out there quick for a handshake."

Everyone stood and started moving about, hugging and shaking hands (but mostly hugging). Molly shrank back in her space at the rear of the sanctuary with her arms crossed.

Hoot vaulted off the platform and hurried down the side aisle. He wrapped his arms around her and whispered, "I didn't think you'd come. Now stick your hand out before those bikers across the aisle come over here lookin' for a feel." And he was gone.

Molly barely heard a word of the sermon. She was awash in emotion and confusion. It must be a sin to feel what she was feeling in church. And about someone who was obviously here to use his considerable talents for the good of the church.

He played and sang several more times during the service. And each time, Molly's only thought was, *how can he be so sexy while he's doing God's work?* No doubt about it, she was going to burn in hell.

The last song Hoot played was "Down By The Riverside". He dragged out the first words, *Gonna lay down my troubles*, low and slow, and paused. There was a collective "Oh, yeah," from the congregation. They were on their feet by the time he continued in his honky-tonk style. His voice had amazing range—from a high wail to a low growl.

Molly was thoroughly turned on. *Now that can't be right,* she told herself. *I think the devil's got a hold of me.*

Chapter 36

When the service was over, Molly found herself in line to greet the minister. As she debated how she could escape the line and avoid the greeting, Hoot stepped up behind her, slipped his arm around her waist and whispered, "Whattaya know. The roof didn't cave in. Although, I thought I felt a tremor when you walked in."

"I'll take that as a compliment."

Before Hoot could answer, they had moved up in line and faced the minister. She greeted Molly, "Good morning. I'm Reverend Camille. Like the hurricane," she added with a sideways glance at Hoot. "Hoot, honey, what's with the ponytail?" Reverend Camille turned away from Molly to focus her full attention on Hoot. She reached up and wrapped her hand around the ponytail that replaced his usual braid.

"Little Em didn't feel like braidin' my hair this mornin'," Hoot answered.

"Is her arthritis acting up again?"

"Seems to be."

"You may soon have to find someone else to do that for you," the minister said, letting the ponytail slide through her fingers.

Molly was beginning to feel superfluous. She made a move to walk away, but Hoot pulled her back. Reverend Camille seemed to notice her again. "You're a new face. I hope you enjoyed the service."

The little devil that sat on Molly's shoulder gave her a jab with his pitchfork. She said, "How could I not? I just came to listen to Hoot."

"Quite an experience, isn't it?" Camille said, studying Molly. "Indeed it is. As you said, he's just full of surprises."

Camille turned back to Hoot. "Will we see you at lunch?"

"Not today."

"Give Emily a hug for me," Camille said. "And tell Oscar I said hello."

"I will," Hoot said. He gave Camille a quick hug and ushered Molly outside.

When they reached her car, Hoot said, "Can I interest you in lunch?"

Molly was rummaging in her handbag for her keys. "What, you're turning down an invitation from the minister to ask me out to lunch?" She found her keys and turned to unlock the door.

Hoot reached out to touch her. "Molly—"

She jerked away. "What was I thinking? I felt like an interloper, while Reverend Hurricane fondled your hair, inquired about your family and basically marked her territory."

Hoot stepped back from her.

"Damn, Molly, I don't think church did you much good. In fact, it seems like the devil got a hold of you."

"Oh, you have no idea," she said. She opened her car door, slid in and drove away with tears in her eyes.

As she drove home, she struggled with the many conflicting images of Hoot. There was the unbelievably talented man, singing and playing the piano, admired and appreciated by the congregation and the way too familiar, in Molly's opinion, Reverend Hurricane; there was the capable, masterful Hoot, who changed her tire and cleaned her gutters; there was the sexy, mysterious Hoot who lured her into his house then walked away from her mid-seduction; and now she was forced to add an image of a childish Hoot sitting at Emily's feet while she braided his long hair (with her arthritic fingers).

~~

134

The blinking light on her answering machine greeted her when she walked in the door. *Now what?* She thought as she pushed the button.

"Molly?"

She recognized Hoot's deep voice and the way he managed to apply a drawl to the two syllables of her name.

"Molly," he repeated, "I've been sittin' here, in the church parkin' lot, on my bike, tryin' to figure out why you're upset. Why would you come to hear me play, then leave mad? And I'm not gettin' any answers. So help me out here. Call me."

The message ended abruptly.

Molly flopped down on the sofa and put her head in her hands. Why was she upset? He had to be kidding. Why would he invite her to church only to have her witness whatever that was between him and Reverend Camille?

Wait, he didn't really invite her. Yes he did, sort of. He just mentioned that he played there and he said "come and see for yourself." And he seemed glad to see her.

Well, she wasn't sure Camille had been glad to see her. The fondling of Hoot's hair, the way she let it be known she was in with his family, obviously knew about Emily's arthritis (something Molly didn't know). In Molly's mind, that was a woman's way of saying to another woman, "I've already staked out this territory, sister."

A memory of Gil's, neat, close-cropped hair flashed in her mind. She reached for the phone to call Richie.

Dennis answered, "Hello, Mollymoms. What's up?"

"What's this about a housewarming party?"

"Oh, yeah. That. I don't know what's gotten into the old man. I'm encouraging him to get a hobby. It's a good thing Richie and I will never have children. Can you *imagine?*"

"In case you couldn't tell, a shudder just went through my body." "How can you say that, Mollymoms? No doubt we would have beautiful, above-average children. If we *could* have children."

"Stop stroking your ego and give me the details about the damn party, Dennis."

"Well, excuuuse me, Mollymoms. Now you've gone and hurt my feelings. Richie," he yelled, "come and talk to my mother-in-law."

Just then, Molly heard the familiar roar of a motorcycle. She peeked through the rectangle of glass in the front door.

"Hello, Mom. What have you done to Dennis? He practically threw the phone at me."

She watched Hoot dismount, lower the kickstand and look up at the house. He squared his shoulders and started up the walk.

"Mom, are you there?"

"Richie, let me call you back in a few minutes." She hung up the phone without waiting for an answer.

Chapter 37

She stepped away from the door and waited for the doorbell. Should she let him in? Did she want to hear his explanations or excuses? Maybe. Did she want him to go away and never bother her again? Maybe not.

What was he doing? He'd surely had time to ring the bell. She cautiously moved back to the door and peeked through the glass. Hoot stood a couple of feet away, his head thrown back, eyes closed, hands at his sides. She watched his chest expand and contract as he breathed deeply.

What was he doing? She sat down and waited.

After what seemed like an eternity, there was a soft knock on the door. Molly thought about ignoring it, but she needed to vent her righteous anger or disappointment, or whatever she was feeling. She got up and opened the door.

Hoot stepped inside. His eyes searched her face. "Molly, help me understand what needs fixin' here and I'll try to fix it." He took a step closer to her.

She backed away. "What were you doing out there before you came to the door? You just stood there, looking at the sky with your ponytail flying in the breeze. You looked like some kind of Indian warrior preparing for battle."

"Work um up courage. Face um pissed off squaw."

"Very funny. Let's start with you and your minister," Molly said, "You know, the little hurricane who likes to fondle your hair and knows way more about Emily than I do."

Hoot looked surprised. "Camille?"

Molly could have sworn she witnessed Hoot having an epiphany. It was either an epiphany or he was an accomplished actor among his many other talents...a slight frown, followed by raised eyebrows and the dawn of understanding in his eyes. "Oh, I see," he said slowly.

"What do you see, Hoot?"

"I see what you think you saw. But it's not like that. Camille is touchy-feely with everyone. It don't mean nothin.'"

Molly ignored the double negative and as she did so, she wondered why Hoot's bad grammar didn't set her teeth on edge.

"How does she know so much about your family?"

"Little Em and Big O both used to be members until she pissed Big O off with a political comment one Sunday. It wouldn't have bothered him if she'd come down on the right side. Literally. But Camille stepped on his political toes. He's a stubborn, unforgivin', old fart."

"What about Emily?"

"She's still a member and goes to church when she feels like it. Tells him he can just stay home and suck his thumb. She's as stubborn as him. Plus her opinion lines up more with Camille's than Big O's."

"Seriously, why were you standing outside the door like that?" Molly asked.

"I believe in the law of mind/action. I was picturin' you not mad at me." After a moment, he went on, "It was a kind of meditation."

Molly was silent as she grappled with yet another image of Hoot. Who was this man?

Hoot said softly, "Molly, talk to me."

"I can't figure you out, Hoot. Are you religious?"

"Prob'ly not the way you're thinkin'," he said. But I'm firm in what I believe. I'm not big on the idea of sin. I don't believe in hell. I believe in heaven on earth." He smiled.

Was that "heaven on earth" bit supposed to be a promise of what he could deliver? Hoot's expression didn't support that theory. He didn't look overly confident and he didn't look like he was making a joke. However, it reminded Molly that she had come close to experiencing heaven on earth in church this morning, before the hurricane hit.

"Now I want to ask you something," Hoot said. "Is your jealousy a sign you want me all to yourself?"

Molly paced back and forth, hands on hips. She finally gave up searching for an appropriately cutting response and said, "I don't know about you, but I'm starving. How about a sandwich?"

Hoot followed her into the kitchen. He sat on a stool at the counter while she put on a pot of coffee and assembled a couple of ham salad sandwiches. She poured two cups of coffee and set the sandwiches on the table. Hoot moved to a chair at the table.

He took a sip of coffee and looked her in the eye. "Thanks. But I'd really like an answer to my question." He took a bite of the sandwich and watched her while he chewed.

Molly picked up her sandwich and laid it back down. "It's complicated," she said. "This morning, watching you play and sing, I was very attracted to you. Turned on actually—I may as well admit it. But there are other issues. I really do find it disturbing that Emily has to take care of your hair. And I wonder if you expect her to cook, clean your house and do your laundry? And I think I may be somewhat uncomfortable with this sudden revelation about your religious leanings. Oh, and I'm too old for you."

Hoot finished chewing and swallowed. He took another sip of coffee and leaned back in his chair. "I do my own laundry. I've got a cute little Merry Maid that comes in once a week to clean my house, but I expect I'll have to let her go—in light of this possessive streak you're showin'."

Molly slammed her fist on the table and glared at him.

"Just kiddin' about the Merry Maid. I clean my own house. There's not that much to clean. I'm not a very messy guy."

The phone rang.

She picked up the kitchen wall phone and glanced at the caller ID. Oops, she forgot to call Richie back. "Sorry, son. I was just about to call you," she lied. "So tell me about this party business."

"Like Dennis said, we don't know what's gotten into Gil. He's a little clingy all of a sudden. So here's the plan. He thinks we're going to have a housewarming party to show off our new digs. But we're really planning a surprise birthday party for him. That's why we want you to have him stay with you. So we can get the house ready without him catching on. We told him the reason he can't stay with us is that we're remodeling the guestroom and—"

"Wait, wait, wait," Molly said. "You want Gil to stay here?"

"Well, yeah. We didn't think it would be a problem. He stayed there when he came for the wedding. And, uh, well, we already told him that was the arrangement."

It occurred to Molly that Dennis would be listening to Richie's side of the conversation and wondering why she didn't want to host his dad again. Damn! The boys didn't know anything about what had happened. As far as they were concerned, she and Gil were nothing more than a couple of old fogies who happened to be their parents. It wouldn't have entered their minds that the old folks needed a chaperone. She took a deep breath.

"Sure. It's no problem. You just caught me by surprise." Molly felt Hoot's eyes on her. Richie was probably wondering if she was getting senile and Dennis was probably feeling hurt. And she felt manipulated. "So," she tried to sound enthusiastic, "when does all this take place?"

"The party's the 12th, a week from next Saturday. That's Gil's birthday. He'll arrive the previous Tuesday, the eighth."

Molly gripped the phone and sat down at the table. "The eighth," she repeated, weakly. "A little over a week from now. Is he flying or driving?"

"He's flying. We'll pick him up at the airport. We should be at your house with him around noon on the eighth."

"The eighth. Around noon. Got it." She pushed the off button and laid the phone down by her plate. "Shit!"

Hoot reached across the table and covered her hand with his. "Is there anything I can do?"

"Not unless you can simplify my life. I've already told you my son is gay. That doesn't bother me, but I've always had to deal with people it did bother. Now my son's partner—no let me just call it like it is—my son's spouse. After all, they got married in California last spring and repeated their vows and had a reception for family and friends two weeks ago. So does that make him my son-in-law? Why don't they have

140

names for this kind of situation? Anyway, his dad—not my son's dad but his spouse's dad is coming to stay at my house for several days."

"That's a little confusing, babe, but I think I understand. So why don't you want the dad to stay here?"

"Oh, God. It's so embarrassing." She looked at her hands, and repeated, "So embarrassing...I almost had sex with Gil when he was here last time. If my sister-in-law hadn't interrupted with a phone call, I'm sure it would have happened. And then barely a week later—" She lost her train of thought for a moment. "I think it's the music. First it was my "Molly Darling" song that got me turned on with Gil. And how the hell do you know that song? You played a snippet of it this morning." She didn't wait for an answer, but charged on. "Then when you played the piano at your house, I would have fallen in bed with you if you hadn't walked away. And why *did* you walk away?"

Once again, she charged on without waiting for an answer. "Oh, and I almost forgot. If it hadn't been for Camille, I would have followed you anywhere this morning after church and done anything you wanted. It must be a reaction to the music. Or maybe I'm just turning into a sex-starved slut."

She stood, picked up her untouched sandwich and threw it in the trash. She hung the phone back in the charger and looked at Hoot with tears in her eyes.

He stood and moved toward her.

"No," she held up a hand to stop him. "That wasn't an invitation. I'm embarrassed and confused." She sat back down at the table, buried her head in her arms, and gave in to the tears.

She heard the sliding door open and close. When she raised her head, Hoot was gone.

Chapter 38

Molly's mood deteriorated as the day went on. She couldn't find a single thing to feel good about.

She wandered into her office and sat down at her desk. Looking for a way to distract herself, she logged on to her computer. She had a message that said, *Hello, Dreamcatcher, One eager new member wants to meet you.*

She clicked on the link, which took her to a small picture of a somewhat dignified-looking man with thinning gray hair and glasses. His handle was amorous1. Another click opened his profile and a larger version of his photo. Before she started to read, she noticed four additional small photos on the left side of the page. An option allowed her to click on them, one at a time, to enlarge the view.

The first photo showed a slender, obviously senior, man lying on his side on a bed, one arm bent at the elbow, his head propped on his hand. The other arm was draped across his waist. He was wearing jeans and no shirt, showing off a pale pigeon chest.

In the second photo, the pose was the same, but he wore only a pair of light blue briefs. The third photo zoomed in on the area of his body from his naval to just below his briefs, facing toward the camera. He was apparently holding his hands above his head so as not to detract from the view of his midsection. The fourth and final photo was a side view of the same area of his body. She assumed this shot had been added to ensure that an impressive bulge under the briefs would not go unnoticed.

"What a fitting end to a totally crappy day," she told her Toshiba laptop. "I've been strip-teased by somebody's grandpa."

She turned off her computer and sat staring at the black screen. She should probably cancel her subscription to Senior Matchmakers. It certainly hadn't done much for her. That train of thought led her to Bob and the disastrous date (if you could call it that) at Best Burgers, which led her to think about Charlie.

What did life have in store for her? Before Gil and Hoot had complicated her life, she had noticed herself viewing every man she saw, who was anywhere near her age, as a potential mate. If she saw a reasonably attractive gray-haired man in the grocery store alone, she surveyed the contents of his shopping cart, trying to determine if he had a wife at home. If he was shopping from a list or getting instructions on his cell phone, he was an unlikely prospect. But if his cart held a stack of frozen dinners and a six-pack, she might discreetly follow him around for a while to see if he noticed her. God, she had been pathetic!

And now that there were two men who seemed interested in her, she had messed that up—at least with Hoot. And she wasn't sure she wanted to think about Gil in those terms again.

After staring at the cold computer screen for several minutes, she got up and left the room. She went to the bookcase that covered one wall of her living room and browsed through the titles. It didn't take long to determine that there wasn't anything there that she hadn't already read or that she was the least bit interested in reading. She sat in her recliner and thought about going to the library, or maybe Barnes & Noble. While she was trying to decide if she wanted to put forth the effort, she nodded off.

~~~

She awoke to the ringing of the phone.

"Molly, it's Jan. I'm out at Independence Center. I'm going to drop by for a minute. Okay?"

"What for?" Molly asked.

But Jan had disconnected. She showed up 20 minutes later, bearing travel brochures. She followed Molly into the kitchen and they sat down at the table. "You got coffee?" she asked.

"Nope," Molly said.

They sat in silence for several minutes. Jan fanned the brochures out on the table in front of Molly. "Surely there's

143

someplace in this exciting sampling of destinations that might interest you."

"Nope," Molly said.

"How about this? I know you're not excited about the Halsteads. So why don't you set up something with Richie and Dennis? I know! If they would like to travel with us, you could see if Gil would like to join us, too."

Several more minutes passed while Molly glared at Jan.

Finally Jan said, "Molly, have you thought about talking to someone?"

"Talking to someone about what?"

"About your depression, Molly. I think you need help."

Molly stood up. "I'm going to go take a nap now. I think that'll help. You can stay as long as you like, but when you leave, take that travel shit with you. And lock the door behind you."

She left Jan sitting at the table with her mouth open and went into her bedroom and slammed the door.

When she was sure Jan was gone, Molly went into the kitchen and rummaged in the refrigerator. She stuffed herself with cookies and milk. It was probably too early to go to bed, but she couldn't think of anything better to do.

She fell asleep with the TV on and dreamed about Sam. In the dream, she had a frantic need to be with him and explain why it had taken her so long to get there.

She searched for her car and couldn't find it. She flagged down a red station wagon and when the driver stopped and opened the door, it was Charlie behind the wheel with a load of squawking chickens in the back.

She turned and ran toward a short, heavyset policeman, screaming, "Help me." He took her arm and led her to a door that said Republican National Headquarters. She broke away and ran from him. He ran after her, calling, "I thought you were intelligent."

She awoke in a tangle of damp sheets with her heart pounding. Sharks swam, silent and menacing, through National Geographic waters on the television screen. The illuminated clock on her bedside table said 3:27 a.m. She clicked off the TV, turned on the lamp and sat up in bed, her eyes wide open, and waited for the dawn.

Once daylight had replaced the dark, frightening night, Molly slid back into bed. She closed her burning eyes and let sleep overtake her.

It was nearly noon when she dragged herself out of the bed. She stumbled into the kitchen and found a box of chocolate covered donuts in the freezer. She ate two of them frozen while she defrosted the remainder of the box.

She craved coffee, but it seemed like too much trouble so she washed down the rest of the donuts with milk. For half an hour, she sat at the table and regarded the empty donut box with a feeling of nausea and self-disgust. She got up and threw the box in the overflowing wastebasket, wondering if it was her or the trash that was getting gamy? Maybe a shower would perk her up.

She stood under the running water and scrubbed herself until her skin felt raw, then scrubbed her scalp until her arms grew tired. After her shower, she sat and stared at the array of potions on her dressing table. When she began to feel like a prune, she applied daytime moisturizer to her face and lotion to the rest of her body. Several minutes passed before she uncapped her deodorant and smeared some under each arm. Finally, she ran a comb through her wet hair, put on some jeans and a tee shirt and left for the grocery store. She had a craving for chocolate chunk ice cream or maybe butter pecan. She couldn't decide so she bought both—and a package of Double Stuff Oreos.

Chapter 39

Late that evening, Liz used her key to let herself into Molly's house. She pulled a kitchen chair into the living room and positioned it directly in front of Molly, where she sat huddled in a corner of the sofa. Liz sat down, planted her feet flat on the floor, her hands on her knees and leaned forward.

"Okay, Molly, you won't answer the phone and you don't return my calls. What's going on?"

Molly glared at her defiantly. "Well?" Liz waited.

"What do you want from me, Liz? I feel like hell. I miss Sam. Jan brought me a stack of travel brochures yesterday and then insinuated I need to see a shrink just because I don't want to go anywhere with her. I wanted to travel but I wanted to do it with Sam, not with Jan and her snooty friends. Oh yeah, I almost forgot. My daughter thinks I'm corrupting my grandchildren with good grammar."

She twisted the bottom of her tee shirt. Tears ran down her cheeks. "My life is shit. I can't find any joy in anything."

"You must be finding some joy in food," Liz observed. "I see you can't button your jeans."

"Boy, if that isn't the pot calling the kettle black," Molly exploded.

"Yeah," Liz said, unperturbed, "but I look cute chubby. You just look fat. And you're going to hate yourself when you have to go shopping for a muumuu to wear to the big party—which, in case you've forgotten, is less than two weeks away."

"So? I have plenty of time to shop for a muumuu. I'm sure Richie and Dennis will take care of every detail of the damned party. As far as I can see, nobody needs me for anything."

"Well, you'd better pull yourself together in time to dust and vacuum the guestroom. It seems like you're needed to play hostess to Gil."

"Yeah, I'm *really* looking forward to that." Her tone said she wasn't. "And what was I thinking when I agreed to that plan. What am I going to do with him for a whole week?"

"There was a time when you liked him," Liz said. "I can't imagine he'll be a lot of trouble. He'll probably be the perfect houseguest. Maybe you two will take up where you left off last time." She stood up and started to haul the chair back into the kitchen. "Then you can forget about the damned biker," she mumbled.

"That's not going to happen."

Liz turned and gave her a strange look. "Which. That you'll take up with Gil again or that you'll forget about the biker?"

"His name is Hoot."

Liz and the chair disappeared into the kitchen. A moment later, she screeched, "My God, Molly. What the hell is this mess in the sink?" She came back into the living room with the offending bowl in her hands.

"It's popcorn, okay? I was craving some popcorn and all I had in the house was that low fat, supposedly butter-flavored shit. It tasted like packing peanuts, so I salted the crap out of it and melted some butter and poured on it. It just turned soggy and I couldn't eat all of it."

"You actually ate *some* of this?" Liz shook her head. She took the bowl back into the kitchen. When she returned, she took Molly's hands in hers and looked into her eyes.

"Molly," she said softly, "will you do something for me?" "What?" Molly was sullen.

"Will you get off your ass and get a grip?"

She pulled Molly to her feet. Then she began to sing, in a gravelly, off-key voice. "Leeen on meee...when you're not strong...and I'll be your friend. . ."

She danced a resistant Molly around the room. "I'll help you care-reee on—"

"Liz?" Molly interrupted.

"Yeah?"

"I'll do anything you say, if you'll stop singing. Or whatever you call that."

Chapter 40

Richie's SUV rolled into Molly's driveway just after 1 o'clock on the appointed Tuesday afternoon. Molly was as ready as she was capable of being. She had pulled herself together after Liz's visit, prepared the guestroom, thrown out the junk food and gone to the store with a healthy food list. She was able to zip and button her jeans this morning.

She stood at the front door and watched as the boys and Gil climbed out and unloaded luggage. Dennis handed Richie a Pullman, picked up a medium-size suitcase and left a duffle bag for Gil. They started up the stairs with their loads. *Ye Gods! How long did he intend to stay?*

She smiled her way through the greetings—a peck on the cheek from Richie, and a slightly strained "Hey, Mollymoms," from Dennis as they slid past her and headed to the guestroom with the luggage. Gil set his bag down and hugged Molly. He followed the hug with an effusion of gratitude at being her guest. He didn't want her to go to any trouble, he really appreciated her hospitality, he was so happy to be here, he felt so comfortable in her home, etc. Dennis returned from the guestroom, took in the scene, picked up Gil's duffle bag and carried it down the hall.

Gil looked tanned and fit. He wore khakis with a sharp crease (did he stand up all the way from Colorado?) a blue knit shirt and brown loafers. His silver hair was short and neat. "Molly," he said, looking her up and down, "you look wonderful."

"Thanks, Gil. Flattery will get you...umm," she felt herself blush "will get you something to drink," she finished lamely. "What would you like? Coffee, tea, Pepsi, Coke? I think I'll have a beer myself." She fled to the kitchen, threw the

148

refrigerator door open and grabbed a Heineken. "Anyone else?" she asked, waving the bottle around.

Dennis was watching her with a strange expression. She thought she saw a glimmer of something in his eyes. She glanced at Richie. Nothing there. Of course not. Richie wouldn't suspect anything if she wore a sign that said, "My, this is awkward, considering Gil and I almost had sex the last time he stayed here."

Gil and Dennis both accepted a beer. Richie declined, "I'm driving," and helped himself to a can of Pepsi. Molly lifted the bottle to her lips and almost choked when she saw Hoot walk onto the deck with a couple of lengths of guttering. He laid them down against the rail and turned and tapped on the door.

Molly watched in shocked disbelief as he slid the deck door open and stuck his head in. "Hey, Molly. Sorry to disturb you. I was gonna replace that leaky downspout today but I see you've got company, so I'll just leave the material and come back later." He nodded to the three men who stood around Molly's table and gave them a friendly smile. "Howdy, I'm Hoot Holcombe, handyman."

Molly felt her face burn. "Sorry, where are my manners?" she murmured. "Hoot, this is my son, Richie, his partner, Dennis, and Dennis's dad, Gil. Guys, this is Hoot Holcombe."

Hoot stepped into the kitchen and shook hands with each of them. "Didn't mean to intrude, Molly."

Like hell, she thought.

"See you later." And he was gone.

She felt them all staring at her. Dennis looked at her over Richie's shoulder and mouthed, *Oops.* He was the only one in the room who seemed at ease. Richie's and Gil's stiff postures suggested they each had a broomstick up their ass.

"How do you know this handyman, Mom?" Richie asked. "I hope you're careful about who you have coming around."

"I, umm, we go to the same church," Molly said.

"Since when do you go to church?"

149

Dennis raised an eyebrow at Molly and laid his hand on Richie's shoulder. "Hey, Richie, we'd better get going. We've got a job to finish up before we come back and take the ancient ones to dinner this evening."

Molly had the thought, not for the first time, that Dennis could turn out to be her favorite child.

She said, "How nice. What time?"

"We'll pick you up at 6:30." And they left.

Gil turned to her and rubbed his palms together. "Ahh," he said, "alone at last."

Molly avoided his eyes. "Have you had lunch?"

"No, but please don't go to any trouble."

"No trouble at all," Molly said. "I thought we might run out to Barnes & Noble. I can check on a book I've been looking for and we can grab a Panini at the Starbucks inside the bookstore."

"Okay, sure." He sounded a little disappointed but quickly recovered. "I love the feel and smell of a bookstore with a coffee shop."

They piled into Molly's car and she headed out Kentucky Road to 291. She felt a lurch in her stomach (or maybe it was her heart) as she rolled past the Holcombe's lane.

"What book are you looking for?" Gil asked.

She pulled her mind back inside the car. Shit. She didn't expect him to ask. "Umm, I want to see if the latest Harley Jane Kozak novel is available," she said, thinking fast. It was sort of true although she hadn't checked Harley Jane's website lately for the status of the book.

"That's an unusual name," Gil said. "I'm not familiar with the author."

"She writes romantic mysteries." Molly went on to describe a little about Harley Jane's first three novels as she turned onto 291 and headed south.

She took the 39th Street exit and turned left into The Commons. She felt that lurch again as she drove past 54th Street Grill, where she and Liz had lunch with Hoot not so long ago.

Hoot. What the hell did the man think he was doing, showing up with guttering today? She hadn't heard from him since the Sunday she went to church. And she had certainly never discussed leaky gutters with him.

Molly told Gil to go ahead and grab a table in the café while she went to chat with an employee behind the circular desk.

When she joined Gil in the café, she gave an elaborate shrug and feigned disappointment. "Not in yet."

They ordered sandwiches and coffee and settled at the table Gil had chosen—the farthest one away from other patrons. Molly was relieved when three women claimed the table closest to them.

Gil watched the women settle at the table, and turned to Molly with a longsuffering smile. "I guess we'll have to wait until we get back to your house to talk," he said.

She didn't answer. What was wrong with her? A couple of months ago, she would have been thrilled at the prospect of being courted by someone like Gil. Why didn't she want that now? Look at him: handsome, well-dressed, smart, well-spoken. *Bet you wouldn't never catch him using no double-negatives*, she thought. She gave herself a mental kick in the ass and resolved to be nice until she figured out what she did want.

On the way home from Barnes & Noble, Molly killed time by driving past some sights of interest, pointing out the Bingham-Waggoner Estate, the National Frontier Trails Museum, The Mormon Temple and the Historic Courthouse on the Independence Square, with its statue of Harry S. Truman. The impromptu tour ended with barely enough time for them to get ready for Richie and Dennis to pick them up for dinner.

Chapter 41

Molly couldn't decide if she was relieved or not that Richie and Dennis turned down the invitation to come in for coffee when they got home from dinner. On one hand, she was nervous about being alone with Gil, but on the other , she didn't feel like extending the evening any longer.

She unlocked the door and stepped out of her shoes as she usually did. Damn. She probably shouldn't have done that. Gil might take it to mean something. She quickly turned to him and said, "Gil, I hope you won't think I'm a terrible hostess, but I have a killer headache and I need to call it a night."

He grabbed her hand as she started to walk away. "I was hoping we could spend some time together tonight. But that's okay. We can talk tomorrow. I want you to be at your best when we talk."

"Thanks for understanding." Molly pulled her hand away. "Make yourself at home. I'll see you in the morning."

She closed and locked her bedroom door, picked up the phone and speed dialed Liz.

"Molly? It's after 11. What's wrong?"

"Oh, God, Liz. I'm a nervous wreck. Gil is determined to get me alone. I don't know what he wants, but I'm not ready for it, whatever it is. And I wouldn't be surprised if Hoot shows up again tomorrow."

She told Liz about his appearance with the guttering. She had no sooner finished the story than she heard a motorcycle slow down, idle for a moment and then race away. "Liz, did you hear that? I'm sure he just buzzed the house. I can't face this alone. Will you come over and spend the day tomorrow, please?"

"Bet your ass! I wouldn't miss this for anything. I'm not sure why the biker's stalking you, but I think we both know what Gil wants. Do you think there'll be a fight?"

Molly hung up.

~~

She stepped out of the shower at 7 a.m., to the sound of someone whistling and the smell of coffee brewing. She pulled her jeans on with one hand and speed-dialed Liz's cell with the other. "Liz, are you on the way?"

"Yes, give me a break. And here's a news flash. I just passed a guy with a ponytail on a black Harley signaling a left turn onto Kentucky from a gravel lane. I hope he's not carrying anything dangerous—like a length of gutter. Nope, didn't see any gutters." She was still laughing when she disconnected.

Molly finished dressing, took a deep breath and walked out of the bedroom. The kitchen blinds and sliding door were open and Gil was on the deck inspecting the gutters. Peaches, the next door neighbor's big, fluffy yellow cat, inspected Gil, who obviously didn't welcome the attention. He made several attempts to push her away with his foot, but Peaches came back, started to purr loudly and rub against his leg. Gil made a scat noise and kicked the cat. She let out a yowl and took off running.

Molly, shocked, had just opened her mouth to chastise Gil when Liz came barging through the front door. "Where's your company?"

"Out on the deck abusing Peaches," Molly said.

"How the hell do you abuse a peach?" Liz asked.

"Peaches is the next door neighbor's cat," Molly answered as Gil came inside.

"Sounds kinky to me," Liz said.

"What's kinky?" Hoot asked as he came through the door right behind Gil.

"Peach abuse," Liz said.

Molly thought Liz was enjoying herself way too much.

Hoot looked from Liz to Molly to Gil and shrugged. "Here," he said, and held out a Tupperware container. "When

Aunt Em heard you had company, she sent you some homemade scones."

Liz grabbed the container and popped the lid off. "I've died and gone to heaven," she chortled. "Someone pour the coffee."

"How nice of her," Molly said. "Hoot, sit down and join us."

Chapter 42

Liz was halfway through her second scone when she snapped her fingers and announced, "I almost forgot. There are a couple of grocery bags full of stuff in the passenger seat of my car. Can one of you hunky guys bring them in?"

Hoot started to rise. Gil jumped up so fast he nearly knocked his chair over. "I'll go." He hurried out the front door.

"Liz," Molly looked at her questioningly, "what's in the bags?"

"Diversionary tools," she stage whispered, behind her hand. "Play along."

Hoot raised an eyebrow and said nothing.

Gil came in with two large brown bags and set them on the table. "Looks like groceries," he said, with a puzzled frown.

"Yeah," Liz said, stuffing the last of the scone into her mouth. "Molly and I talked about how it'd be fun to make our famous meatballs and spaghetti for you and the boys while you're here." She jumped up and started unloading the sacks. "It's been a long time since we made them. Probably because they're a real pain in the ass to make. Takes all damn day. But I know Richie and Dennis will be thrilled. Gil, it's your lucky day. You can even help. It'll be fun.

"Molly, call Richie and tell him and Dennis to haul their asses over here at 6:30 this evening. And tell them to bring beer. I'll call Joe." She turned and gave Hoot an appraising look. "You might as well stay, too, biker dude. We'll have a party!"

Finally, Liz raised her hands to the ceiling and intoned, "God bless the meatballs and spaghetti—and God bless the meatballs and spaghetti makers. Let us begin."

Molly slid her look around the room. Gil was open-mouthed, shaking his head, with a *what-the-hell* expression on his face.

Hoot pressed his lips together and fished a piece of plastic straw out of his pocket to chew on. "Molly," he said around

155

the straw, "you oughta hang onto this woman. I know I would."

Liz tilted her head to one side, batted her eyes at Hoot and said, "Yeah, baby. Guess you can tell—there's a lotta woman packed into these 220 pounds."

Gil divided a death ray glare between Hoot and Liz.

"Okay, Liz," Molly said. "Let's go to the basement and see if we can find my spaghetti sauce cauldron. It's been a while since I used it." She grabbed Liz by the arm and hustled her to the basement door.

Molly stopped at the bottom of the basement stairs and turned to Liz. "Oh, my God, Liz. What was that all about? I thought you didn't approve of Hoot. Now you're not only inviting him to stay all day—you're flirting with him!"

"Don't give me any shit. If I have to stay here and cook all day, it might as well be entertaining. Do you think they'll get in a fight?"

Molly shook her head. "I'm pretty sure there's something wrong with you, Liz. But thanks." Her eyes filled with tears as she hugged Liz. "Hoot's right. I'm gonna hang on to you."

"Don't get all mushy on me. I'm just trying to live vicariously through your fairy moan experiences."

"My what?"

"You know, that animal chemical thing you've been releasing. Now we'd better find your cauldron and get back up there before Gil pops a vessel. I don't want to miss anything."

Within 30 minutes, Molly's kitchen was teeming with activity. Liz was clearly in charge, barking assignments while she bustled about mixing the ground beef with eggs, breadcrumbs and grated cheese. She nagged at Molly to hurry up with the onion she was dicing.

Gil was assigned to open cans of tomato juice and tomato paste and empty them into the cauldron. When Molly finished with the onion, Liz added it to the ground beef and stuck her hands in the bowl to mix everything by squishing it through her fingers. Molly set a huge skillet on the stove and added shortening.

Liz announced, "It's time to start browning balls. Can either of you hunky men squeeze balls into a uniform size?"

Gil looked at the bloody mixture in the bowl, picked up the morning newspaper and retreated to the recliner in the living room. "If you need something lifted, call me."

Hoot stepped up to the bowl. "What size balls?"

Liz formed a small meatball and showed him. "Not too big. About like this, okay?"

Hoot grinned. "Okay, I can make little balls. I'm secure in my manhood."

The recliner creaked, the newspaper rattled and Gil harrumphed.

Hoot proved himself not only able to make meatballs of a perfectly consistent size, but also to keep up with the assembly line process. Liz placed the meatballs in the skillet to brown. Molly took the browned meatballs from the skillet and placed them in the cauldron of sauce. Hoot stayed with it until the last meatball was browned and added to the sauce.

"Man, that's a lotta meatballs and sauce," he said. "How many people are you plannin' to feed?"

"No telling," Liz said. "It's been our experience that hoards of people magically show up when we make our . . ." Molly and Hoot chimed in to join Liz, "famous meatballs and spaghetti."

There was a loud "harrumph" and rattle of newspaper from the living room.

Molly said, "Liz, remember when Joe's mom finally gave you the recipe?"

"Yeah, the old bitch. At the end of the instructions, she wrote, 'Don't forget to cook some spaghetti.' My own sweet mama, God rest her soul, told me I should never speak ill of the dead. So when his mom died, I said GOOD."

It was close to noon when the smell of meatballs simmering in the sauce filled the house and caused stomachs to grumble. Gil returned to the kitchen to peek in the cauldron. "What happens now?" he asked. "It looks like everything's done and it didn't take all day, after all."

"Oh, our work is not done," Liz said. The sauce has to simmer all afternoon and must be watched closely. Then we'll have to

157

cook a lot of spaghetti and toast a lot of Italian bread with garlic butter. It'll be hours before we can eat. I know, let's order a pizza for lunch."

There was a commotion in the living room—three short buzzes of the doorbell followed by the sound of the lock turning. The door banged open and two rambunctious boys burst in ahead of their mother.

Sophie yelled at the boys. "Gus! Zach! Settle down. Whoa, Mom! Do I smell meatballs? I hope you were planning to call us."

Suddenly everyone was in the kitchen and all talking at once.

Gus: "Whose bike is that in the driveway?"

Zach: "Hi, Gil. Did you ride all the way here from Colorado on that bike?"

Sophie: "Hi, Gil. We heard you were here and thought we'd see if you and Mom wanted to go to lunch. Liz, if I hadn't recognized your car, I'd figure the Harley belonged to you."

As the chaos ebbed, they all seemed to notice Hoot. Zach stepped closer to him and said, "I'll bet that's your bike. You're the only one here that looks like a biker. I'm Zach. That's my brother, Gus and my mom, Sophie. Molly's my grandma." He stuck out his hand.

Hoot shook his hand and smiled. "You guessed right. It's my bike. I'm Hoot. Your grandma's, umm, handyman. I came over to fix the downspouts and got roped into helping with the meatballs."

Gil harrumphed again. "Yeah, turns out Hoot is a pretty good little kitchen helper."

Molly glanced at Hoot, expecting an angry reaction but his expression was neutral. She narrowed her eyes and shot a look at Gil. He gave no indication that he noticed.

Liz to the rescue: "Sophie, we were just getting ready to order pizza and you guys were getting ready to go to lunch. We have to stay here and watch the sauce. Makes sense you have pizza with us then hang around for our famous . . ." everyone except Gil chimed in, "meatballs and spaghetti."

"Great!" Sophie said. "I'll call Myron and tell him what's up. He can come straight here from work."

"I'll call in the pizza order," Molly said, "since Zach so capably handled the introductions." She retreated to her bedroom to escape the high decibel level and ordered three large pizzas, one pepperoni, one meat lovers and one cheese. When she came out of the bedroom, the house was strangely silent. There was nobody in sight except Gil, who lurked at the end of the hall waiting for her.

"Where is everyone?" she asked him.

"They're all out in the driveway admiring the Harley," Gil said. "And Hoot is offering to give piano lessons to Gus." He shoved his hands deep into his pockets. Cords stood out on his neck and Molly thought his face was too red to be healthy. "Is there anything that fucker can't do? Or claim he can do?"

Molly stared at Gil. "Why are you so upset?"

"Molly, it's like Grand Central Station around here. How many people have keys to your house? They just let themselves in like they own the place. I can't even get a few minutes alone with you so we can talk."

Her reply was cut off by the tide of humanity swarming back into the house. "Grandma, guess what!" Gus yelled. "Hoot is gonna teach me to play the piano."

"Really?" She glanced at Sophie in time to see the eye roll.

"I don't know why it has to be piano," Sophie said. "I was trying to talk him into drums."

"Well, a piano really makes more sense," Molly said. "You already own a piano and a set of drums would cost a bundle."

She escaped to the kitchen to check on the sauce with Sophie right behind her. She thought, *here it is again. Richie played the piano; therefore the piano is for sissies.* She rounded on Sophie and hissed, "Why the resistance to Gus learning piano? If you think it's not manly enough, honey, you haven't heard Hoot play the piano."

Molly and Sophie stared at each other. It was hard to say which one was more surprised at Molly's words. After a moment, Sophie planted her hands on her hips and a big smile on her lips. "Okay, Mom, just how handy is your handyman? Hmmm?"

That was the scene Liz walked in on. She looked from one to the other and said, "Uh oh." She took the big spoon from Molly's hand, stirred the sauce and started to sing in her gravelly, off-key voice, "Twas a moment like this...do you remember—"

Gil poked his head in and went "Pssst" at Sophie. "Are you sure Hoot is qualified to give piano lessons?"

Sophie smothered a laugh behind her hand and said, "Mom thinks so. Why don't we find out?" She fairly skipped into the living room. "Hey, Hoot! Let's dust off Mom's neglected piano and you can play us a tune. I want to interview Gus's potential teacher."

"Yeah," Gus said. That'd be cool. Maybe we could even start my lessons now."

Gil leaned against the kitchen archway with his arms crossed and a smug look on his face. Molly and Liz left the sauce and brushed by him to see what Hoot would do. Liz tossed a dishtowel to Sophie. Sophie lifted the lid on the old piano and ran the dishtowel over the yellow keys.

All eyes turned to Hoot.

"It hasn't been tuned since Richie left home," Molly said nervously.

Hoot stepped up to the piano, flexed his fingers and pulled out the bench. He sat down and looked over his shoulder. "Any requests? And please be kind."

Gil yelled, "How about 'Chantilly Lace'?"

"Ooh, not sure I know that one," Hoot said.

A smirk attached itself to Gil's face.

Hoot rolled his shoulders and ran his fingers over the keys. He tentatively picked out a few notes. When it was beginning to sound recognizable as "Chantilly Lace", he hummed a few bars, scooted the bench back a little, and tore into the song like Jerry Lee Lewis on steroids. He pounded out the music and sang, "Chantilly Lace and a pretty face, and a pony tail..."

There was surprised delight on every face except one.

When Hoot sang the lines, "feel real loose, like a long-neck goose," he stretched his neck from side to side and had the boys gasping with laughter. Then he dropped his voice to a sexy bass for the line, "Oh, baby, that's-a what I like."

Sophie and Liz stood side by side. Liz had her hand over her heart and Sophie mock fanned herself with both hands. Molly raised her eyebrow at them and returned to the kitchen.

As she passed Gil, he muttered something that sounded like, "I suppose the fucker can walk on water, too."

Molly smiled at him. "Do you have another request?"

"Yeah, I'd like for him to play far, far away."

~~

By 6:30 Molly's house was bursting at the seams.

Liz had just called "come and get it" when the doorbell rang and Jan burst through. "I wondered what all the cars were doing out front. Molly! I smell meatballs and spaghetti. I haven't had yours and Liz's famous meatballs and spaghetti since Arnie died. I guess you tried to call me and I wasn't home. You should have called my cell. Oh, my God. Is that Gil I see?"

~~

Gil filled his plate and managed to claim the recliner before anyone else could get there.

When Jan came into the living room with her plate piled high, she pulled the piano bench in front of the recliner. She straddled the bench with her plate between her knees.

Liz poked Molly with her elbow. "Would you just look at that?" She nodded toward the spectacle that was Jan on the make.

They watched Jan pull one strand of spaghetti loose with her fork and slowly suck it into her pursed lips. The end finally disappeared into her mouth with a sloppy smacking sound. She then speared a meatball and held it up on her fork while she slowly licked the sauce off it. When she had licked the meatball clean, she wrapped her tongue around it and sucked it into her mouth where she held it for a moment before she chewed.

Gil had stopped eating and stared at her. Molly wondered if it was fascination or fear.

Gus sidled up to Molly and whispered, "Grandma, is Aunt Jan trying to be sexy or does she just have really bad manners?"

Chapter 43

Molly had just turned on the coffee maker the next morning when Gil came into the kitchen looking freshly scrubbed and smelling like soap and shampoo. He wore blue jeans with a crease ironed into them and a plaid cotton shirt open over a white tee shirt. His tennis shoes were blindingly white.

"Good morning, Molly, darling," he said.

Molly gritted her teeth. "Morning, Gil. Sorry I deserted you again last night. By the time everyone left, I was wiped out. Did you sleep well?"

"Like a log. Don't worry about last night. Today is ours." He strolled over to the patio doors and opened the vertical blinds.

"Good God, Molly!" he gasped. "There's a stranger sleeping on your deck."

Molly came to the door and looked out. Hoot was curled on his side in a fetal position on the chaise. The collar of his black denim jacket was turned up against the cool morning air. His head was pillowed on his right arm and his left arm was draped over a big yellow cat.

"He's a little strange," Molly said, shaking her head, "but he's no stranger."

She unlocked the door and slid it open. The next door neighbor's cat, Peaches, untangled herself and stretched lazily. Hoot opened one eye, looked at Molly, and sat up.

"Hoot, what the hell are you doing?" Molly demanded.

"Mornin', Molly. I thought I'd get an early start on the downspouts. It's supposed to rain today. But it didn't look like anyone was up and I didn't want to disturb you, so I thought I'd wait until there was a sign of life before I started poundin'. Didn't mean to doze off." He absently stroked the purring cat as he spoke.

Molly could feel Gil's breath on her neck. He cleared his throat as if to get her attention. She turned to him. He stepped back from the door a little and whispered, "Do you want me to get rid of him?"

Molly was so annoyed she could have strangled both men and barbequed the cat. Well, maybe she'd spare the cat. "What do you mean get rid of him?" She hissed. "Of course not."

She turned back to the door and said to Hoot, "The coffee's done. You may as well come on in."

Hoot came inside. "Howdy, Gil." He stuck out his hand. Gil ignored it, coughed and moved to a chair on the other side of the round table, putting the entire 60 inches of table between them.

Hoot looked at his hand and said, "Guess I oughta wash my hands. Can I use your bathroom, Molly?"

"Sure. Down the hall on your right." She set three cups on the table and poured coffee. When Hoot returned to the table, he took a chair near Molly.

Gil stirred sugar and cream into his coffee with a little more clatter than necessary, in Molly's opinion. Hoot took a sip of his black coffee and smiled, first at her and then at Gil. "So, do you have big plans for today? Molly, are you gonna show Gil around town?"

Gil laid down his spoon and glared at Hoot. "Actually, I was hoping for some quiet time. There are some things I want to discuss with Molly."

"Well, don't let me get in the way," Hoot said cheerfully. "I'll just finish my coffee, get those downspouts replaced and be outa here. Shouldn't take me much past noon."

Gil set his cup down so hard coffee sloshed out.

Molly got up and brought paper towels to the table. She felt her hackles rising. This was her house, her table, her coffee and her downspouts. It seemed like there was a game in progress, and she was the only one not getting a turn to play.

"You boys can do what you want to," she said, throwing the soppy paper towels into the trash. "But I'm hungry." She took bacon, eggs and butter from the refrigerator and laid them on the counter next to the stove. "Who wants breakfast?"

"But Molly, I was going to take you out for breakfast," Gil objected.

"Sorry, Gil. I'm not up to it. I'm eating here. Who's joining me? Hoot, did you have breakfast before you came over?"

"Well, no, but...I wouldn't think of—"

Molly turned to him with a strip of bacon in her hand. "And I wouldn't think of sending you out to replace my gutters on an empty stomach." She filled the frying pan with bacon and began to crack eggs into a bowl. "I hope everyone likes scrambled." She plucked a whisk out of a jar on the counter and started vigorously beating the eggs. After a moment, she looked up to see both men watching her. Maybe she was putting a little too much oomph into the beating.

Gil sat back in his chair with his arms crossed and his chin tucked down to his chest. Hoot had his chair turned partially toward her, his posture relaxed, his hands at rest on his thighs.

She set the bowl of eggs down, picked up a fork to turn the bacon and let out a yelp as it popped and spattered on her arm. "Shit, shit, shit!"

Hoot got to his feet, lowered the burner, took the fork from her hand and began turning the bacon. Gil rose halfway out of his chair, sputtering, "Molly, are you okay? Shall I get you a Band-Aid? I knew we should have gone out."

"I'm fine," Molly said, tightly.

Gil sat back down.

Hoot slid past Molly and opened cupboards until he found a platter. He watched over the bacon until it was done. He reached around Molly to pull paper towels off the dispenser and placed them on the platter before

164

dishing up the bacon. Molly put bread in the four-slice toaster, emptied the bacon grease into a can and poured the eggs into the skillet. Hoot buttered toast and reloaded the toaster while Molly stirred the eggs. The eggs and toast were done at the same time.

Would have worked like clockwork, Molly thought, *if someone had set the table instead of pouting.* She glanced at Gil, glued to his seat, staring hatred at Hoot, who was already taking plates out of the cupboard and pulling drawers open looking for silverware.

When they were seated, Hoot passed the eggs to Molly. She took some and passed them to Gil. He helped himself and set the bowl down without passing it on to Hoot. Hoot smiled, passed the bacon to Molly and half stood to reach across the table for the eggs. Molly couldn't believe her eyes when Gil repeated the rude slight with the bacon.

She said, "Gil, would you mind passing the bacon to Hoot?"

"Sorry," he mumbled, and gave the platter a shove that sent it skidding across the table. Hoot caught it just before it crashed into his plate. "Much obliged," he said, mildly. He slid a couple of strips of bacon onto his plate. His expression remained benign.

"What kind of work do you do, Gil?" Hoot asked pleasantly.

"I'm retired."

"Lucky you." Hoot picked up a strip of bacon and took a bite.

"One might assume you're retired, too, Gil said, "seeing as how you seem to have so much free time."

Hoot smiled and offered Gil the plate of toast.

Gil ignored it. "What's your real name? It must feel silly to be called Hoot."

Hoot set the toast down. "It's Harvey."

Gil snorted. "I'll bet that was a real bully magnet when you were a kid."

Molly was shocked at the escalation of Gil's rudeness. But Hoot seemed impassive.

He said, "Not really. I didn't put up with a lot of bullying."

Gil laughed. "What did you do? Play the piano at 'em?"

Hoot's white teeth flashed in the widest smile Molly had seen on him. He leaned toward Gil and propped his right elbow on the table, hand open. He said, in a soft voice, "Wanna arm wrestle?"

Molly gasped. Gil stared at Hoot. After a long moment, he moved around the table to the chair on Hoot's right and propped his arm in the wrestling stance. They grasped each other's hands.

"On the count of three?" Gil asked.

"Just say when you're ready and go for it," Hoot said.

There was a long silence while the two men took each other's measure. Finally, Gil shouted, "Ready!" and the next nanosecond his arm hit the table so hard the breakfast dishes jumped.

"How about another go?" Gil asked. "It's hard to make the call and focus at the same time."

"Understood," Hoot said mildly. "How about if Molly counts. Go on three."

"That'll work." Gil made a production of resetting himself in the chair, flexing his hand. Hoot sat motionless, waiting."

Molly said, "Okay, one more time and that's it. I'm going to turn my back and count to three. If it's a draw, then it will remain undecided. No best two out of three. I don't want my house destroyed by a bunch of little boy posturing. Tell me when you're both ready."

They got into position and gave her the nod. She turned her back and counted. "One, two, three." Slam! She turned around to see Gil's arm flattened beneath Hoot's.

Hoot stood and offered his hand in a sportsmanlike gesture, which Gil ignored. "Better get on those downspouts before the rain starts. Sorry to leave you with the cleanup, Molly. But I'm sure Gil will help." He turned and slipped through the sliding door.

Molly looked at Gil. She almost felt sorry for him. Hoot had humiliated him with the same ease with which he did everything. True, Gil had asked for it. In fact, he had been asking for it for two days. It was a wonder Hoot had taken the abuse as long as he did.

She started clearing the table. Gil looked up and said, "I can't prove it and I can't figure out how, but I think he cheated. He made a fool of me didn't he?"

Molly said, "Forget about it. Let's go for a drive. Maybe walk through Burr Oaks, like last time you were here."

"What about *him*. Are you just going to leave him here?"

"Why not? I'll tell him we're leaving. He'll probably be finished and gone by the time we get back."

"If only!" Gil mumbled.

Molly went outside and slid the door shut behind her. Hoot was high up on a ladder removing the old downspout. She waited until he came down and told him about her plan to take Gil to Burr Oaks.

"Babe, I can't believe you came close to sleepin' with him. I guess I oughta say I'm sorry about the arm wrestlin', but I'd be lyin'. He had it comin'."

Molly smiled. "He thinks you cheated."

"Do you?"

"No, but sometimes I think you're supernatural."

"That's funny. I think you and Liz have supernatural powers. I'll bet you wanted to be Wonder Woman when you were a little girl."

Molly laughed. "Yeah, sometimes—when I wasn't Sheena, Queen of the Jungle. They both had really cool outfits."

"If you were Wonder Woman or Sheena, what was Liz?" "Same as now. Loyal sidekick."

"Where's your cell phone, Wonder Woman?"

"In my pocket."

"Let me see it." He took it from her and punched buttons. "Push nine for my cell number if you need anything."

Chapter 44

Molly parked at the mouth of the Bethany Falls Trail and started to get out of the car.

Gil wrapped his hand around her arm to stop her. "Wait, Molly. Can we just sit here in the car and talk for a bit?"

Molly closed the car door and turned to him. "I'm listening."

"Well! Where to start?" He seemed nervous. "I thought we would have had this conversation a lot sooner. Molly, I don't remember your house being so busy before. I've been trying to get a few moments alone with you for two days."

"We're alone now, Gil," Molly said.

He turned toward her and took her hand. He cleared his throat. "I've been thinking about this ever since we were together after the wedding. It makes so much sense. We can be one big family. Dennis loves you, and I think Richie is fond of me. My life with Louise was not a happy one. I'm not getting any younger and I know you would make me happy for my remaining years."

Molly was dumbfounded. She had expected Gil to complain about Hoot. She had even expected him to try and get into her pants. But she had not expected this.

Gil smiled shyly and continued. "You haven't said anything. I suppose this is a real surprise. Anyway, think about it. I have my house in Colorado Springs. We could live there and visit here. Or I guess we could live here. But it would sure be a lot more peaceful in Colorado Springs, away from all the chaos here.

And there's no denying the physical attraction between us. I keep remembering our dance and the kiss."

Molly had turned the car off before this conversation started and it became hotter than hell. She said, "Gil, I need some air. I don't know what to say. I don't even know where to begin.

169

I'm going to walk." She pulled her keys out of the ignition, opened the door and started up the path.

Gil got out of the car and caught up with her. "You don't have to give me an answer right now. I know I sprung it on you."

Molly stopped and turned to him. "Give you an answer? To what? Exactly what are you asking?"

"Why, I'm asking you to marry me, of course." He wrapped his arms around her and pulled her close. When he kissed her, she tensed up. He pulled back and looked at her. "Am I moving too fast, darling?"

She extricated herself from Gil's embrace and stepped back. "I...I need a few minutes alone. Please wait at the car or else walk the other path. They both come back to the same place.

She turned and walked very fast until she came to the first overlook. She stepped off the path and across the footbridge. When she was certain Gil hadn't followed her, she leaned against the rail and pulled her cell phone out of her pocket. She needed to talk to Liz. She meant to call Liz, but—

He answered on the first ring. "Molly, what's wrong?"

"Oh my God, Hoot. He asked me to marry him." She was breathing hard from walking so fast.

"What did you say?"

"I told him I needed to be alone and ran away. When he kissed me, I thought about you. How could that be? You've never even kissed me."

"Babe," his voice was husky, "that's some unfinished business we need to take care of. Do you want me to come and get you?"

"No, I don't know why I called you. I meant to call Liz."

"It was your subconscious. I can be there in a flash."

"No. I'll handle it. If he tries anything, I'll kick him so hard he won't be able to tell his gonads from his eyeballs."

"God, I love it when you talk dirty."

Molly retraced her steps and found Gil leaning against the hood of her car with his arms crossed. "Didn't you walk?" she asked.

"No, I didn't need to clear my mind. I'm already certain." He looked so self-satisfied Molly wanted to tie him to a tree and drive off without him. But she'd probably have a hard time explaining that to Dennis.

She put her hands on her hips and took a deep breath. "Gil, please understand. I'm nowhere near ready for such a step. I'm sorry if you—"

"Darling," he interrupted, "just take a couple of days to let it settle in your mind. Then we can make the announcement at the housewarming party Saturday. Won't everyone be surprised?"

"Excuse me," Molly blurted. "Nature calls." She ran for the outhouse that sat at the edge of the woods. She threw open the door and jumped inside without bothering to check for spiders. She banged her head with her fist and waited for the nausea to pass. After several minutes, she emerged from the outhouse and returned to her car.

"Sorry, Gil. I seem to have developed a case of the scoots," she lied. "I need to get home and take some pink stuff. Let's go."

Chapter 45

Hoot's Harley was still in the driveway. Gil let out a long sigh and said, "Jesus, Molly. You need to charge him rent."

Molly released her own long sigh. *Two more days*, she thought, *and I can hand him off to Dennis and Richie.*

Another car pulled into the driveway beside Molly's. Sophie and the boys jumped out. "Hey, Grandma," Gus yelled. Hoot's gonna give me my first piano lesson today." He and Zach darted up the steps and into the house.

"Mom," Sophie said, "I hope you don't mind. Actually, Hoot suggested it. He thought we'd be more comfortable doing it here to start with, seeing as how we don't know him that well."

Gil rolled his eyes. "Molly, what about your stomach problem? Do you really feel up to all this right now?"

Sophie gave Molly a questioning look. Molly draped her arm around Sophie's shoulder and frowned at Gil, "Please, Gil, don't concern yourself with my stomach problem. I'm feeling much better now that I'm home."

"Where've you been?" Sophie asked.

"We went for a walk out at Burr Oaks. Gil needed some exercise and fresh air."

"Actually," Gil said, "what I needed was a few minutes alone with Molly. But then she developed this...this stomach problem." He stomped up the steps and left them standing in the driveway.

Sophie turned to Molly. "Mom, it sounds like this isn't a good time. I'll tell Hoot we need to reschedule."

"Sophie, if you leave me here with that man, I'll cut you out of the will."

"Which man?"

"Gil," Molly hissed. She heard the scales being played on the piano and dragged herself up the steps to face the music. Literally.

Hoot looked up and winked at Molly. Gus sat beside him on the piano bench, his face aglow. "Look, Mom, he said as Sophie walked in." He executed a halting rendition of the scales.

"I think we've got us a natural here," Hoot drawled.

Gus beamed.

Gil went out the sliding door with a Heineken in his hand.

I guess it's afternoon somewhere, Molly thought.

Zach stretched out on the couch with his nose in the latest *Harry Potter* book.

Sophie took a few steps down the hall and motioned Molly to follow her. They slipped quietly into Molly's bedroom. Sophie plumped pillows up behind her back and made herself comfortable. She waited for Molly to do the same.

"Okay, Mom. I'm a big girl now. Spill."

Molly's heart swelled with love for Sophie. Her little girl was indeed a big girl now—and a very perceptive one.

"I don't know, sweetie," she said. "This is normally Liz stuff. Are you sure you want me to unload it on you."

"You bet. You used to listen to my boyfriend problems. It's time for a little role reversal. So unload already."

And Molly unloaded. She told Sophie about the moment with Gil after the reception. She told her about Jan's call that interrupted the moment and about Gil's sudden departure.

Sophie interjected, "Skinny bitch."

She told her about meeting Hoot. She told her how his music turned her on. This elicited an, "Ooh, la, la, Mama Mia," from Sophie.

She told her how Hoot seemed to have psychic powers the way he figured out that she and Liz were together at 54th Street Grill. She told her how Hoot had been showing up with phony excuses ever since Gil arrived. She ended by telling her about Gil's proposal.

That's when Sophie jumped off the bed and paced. "Let me get this straight. He talked about how miserable his life with his wife had been. And that somehow makes him deserve to have you spend the rest of your years making the rest of his years happy. He wants you to fill a hole in his life. He wants to take you away to live in Colorado so he doesn't have to put up with the chaos of your family. Is that about it? Did he ever mention what was in it for you? How is this happy union he's dreamed up supposed to enrich your life? He sounds to me like an insufferable control freak."

She stopped pacing and looked down at Molly with her hands on her hips. "Do you want me to kill him?" she said in a frighteningly reasonable tone. "I'll bet Hoot and Liz would help me hide his body."

Molly burst out laughing. She jumped up and hugged Sophie. "God, I love you. Wait 'til I tell Liz how great you've turned out!"

There was a knock on the door. Molly realized the piano had stopped. A tentative voice came through the door. "Mom? Grandma? Is everything all right in there?"

Molly opened the door. Zach stood with a finger holding his place in his book, a concerned look on his face. "Everything's fine." She ruffled his hair and followed him into the living room.

Hoot gathered up sheet music.

Gus strutted around with newfound importance.

Gil sat at the table on the deck with a full Heineken and a couple of empties in front of him.

Molly noticed Sophie hadn't followed her out of the bedroom. When she finally emerged, she had a cat-that-ate-the-canary-look about her.

Hoot glanced at the scene on the deck with a worried expression. "Molly, I need to deliver a computer, but maybe I shouldn't leave right now."

Sophie sidled up to him and said, "Don't worry, Hoot. I've got it covered."

The phone rang. Sophie grabbed it and sang out, "Gil, it's for you." She slid the door open and handed the phone to him. After a short conversation, he came inside and handed the phone to Molly.

"Richie wants to talk to you."

174

Molly took the phone. "Richie, what's up?"

"Dennis and I are coming to get Gil. Sophie tells me you and Liz need to go shopping with her for something for the party. She was afraid Gil would be bored there alone. So we're going to show him around our current remodel. Be there in a few."

Molly disconnected and the phone rang again before she could hang it back on the wall.

"Molly," Liz shouted, "I'll be there in 15 minutes."

Sophie was in the corner on her cell phone. She flipped it shut and called to the boys. "Gus, Zach, get your stuff together. Grandma and Grandpa Crandall are on the way to pick you up. You're going to stay with them while I go shopping with Grandma Molly and Liz. And the uncles are coming to get Gil," she added in a low voice as she skirted around Molly and Hoot.

Gil rejoined his Heineken on the deck.

Hoot stepped close to Molly and whispered in her ear, "How did she know they were coming after Gil? I think Wonder Woman's got a Wonder Daughter." Molly followed his gaze to where Sophie stood, hands on hips, commanding the action. She caught them watching her and cast a brilliant smile their way.

"You may be right," Molly said.

"And, babe, we've got some unfinished business." The tip of his tongue brushed her ear lobe for the merest second. Her insides trembled and her knees felt rubbery.

"Call if you need me," he said, his lips still against her ear. "I'll see you tomorrow." And he was gone.

Everyone showed up at the same time, as if they had formed a caravan for the trip to Molly's house. Richie and Dennis parked on the street, Liz pulled in behind them and Grandma and Grandpa Crandall brought up the rear. Gil dragged himself away from his station on the deck and looked out front.

"Christ, I can't wait to spend some time at a peaceful construction site," he mumbled as Dennis and Richie came through the door. Dennis gave him a strange look and then glanced quickly at Molly. She felt bad for her son-in-law and wanted to say something to him, but chaos took over again as Liz and the Crandalls crowded in behind Richie and Dennis.

It took another 10 minutes for everyone to clear out except Molly, Liz and Sophie.

"I'll drive," Liz announced, and they all piled into her car. Molly sank back in the front passenger seat and sighed. "Wow, I'm exhausted. Not sure how much energy I have for shopping. Besides, I've already got Gil's gift. I put together an album of the wedding pictures for him."

"Not a problem," Sophie giggled. We're not going shopping. We're going to have a long lunch, with alcoholic content, and make sure we get all of your stuff out in the open."

"Fuckin' A," Liz shouted, and with some effort turned her chubby body halfway around to execute a high five with Sophie, who sat in the back seat.

They went to V's, where they had Bloody Marys *before* lunch and a bottle of wine *with* lunch.

When every detail of Molly's story had been laid out, examined and re-examined, Liz said, "Okay, I hate to say I was wrong, so I won't. I'm almost never wrong but I may have been under-informed." She gave Molly a look that was full of accusation. "I would have caught on anyway. I was beginning to see a little unattractive side of Gil the last few days. And I have to say your biker is lookin' better all the time. Damned if he isn't. Whew! She fanned herself with both hands. That dude sure can tickle the keys on a piano!"

Sophie giggled. "I think he tickled Mom's ear with his tongue a while ago, right in front of everyone. Well not in front of Gil, who was chugging beer on the deck. But somehow I don't think that would have stopped him."

"I don't think it would have either," Molly said. "Hoot has had just about enough of Gil." And she told them about the arm wrestling incident.

"Woohoo!" Liz and Sophie slapped another high five across the table.

Molly said, "Sophie, now that I've laid out my true confessions, it's your turn. I'm pretty sure you orchestrated Gil's removal from the house. How'd you do it?"

"First, I called Richie and told him what he said I told him—that we needed to go shopping and they should come after Gil. I also told him I'd relieve him and Dennis both of their gay gonads if they ever dumped Gil on you again. Then I hung up. So I'll have some explaining to do somewhere down the line. But I'm up to it." Another high five across the table and wine glasses teetered. "Then I called Liz and told her to get her ass over to your house if she didn't want to miss the excitement."

Molly held up her hand and said, "Stop," before they could high five again.

"Now, here's the plan," Sophie continued. "I'm going to call the guys and tell them not to bring Gil back until late tonight. You'll already be in bed, with your door locked, and they'll tell him not to disturb you. And Hoot will be back early in the morning."

"When did you talk to Hoot?"

"I didn't. But I'm willing to bet."

"You're acting like Gil's a homicidal maniac," Molly said. "He's a pain in the ass, but I really don't think my life is in danger."

"That depends on how much shit you can stand before you slit your wrists," Liz said.

Chapter 46

Molly emerged from her bedroom the next morning, quietly, barefoot, with her hair still damp from the shower. She tiptoed into the kitchen and listened for sounds from the guestroom. She hoped Gil was still asleep or better yet, that the boys hadn't brought him back. She didn't hear him come in last night.

She longed for an hour without his presence. But no such luck. She heard the shower in the bathroom down the hall. Damn.

She had just started the coffee brewing when there was a light tap on the sliding door. She opened the vertical blinds. Hoot stood there with her newspaper in his hand.

She slid the door open. "My, you're early this morning. What are you up to today? Piano lessons, downspouts?"

He laid the newspaper on the table. "Unfinished business, babe. Where's your houseguest?"

"Sounds like he's in the shower," she said as she reached up to take three coffee mugs from the cupboard. When she turned around, she found herself in Hoot's arms.

"Damn, you smell good," he said. He trapped her against the counter and nuzzled her neck. He ran his tongue along her jaw line, to her ear lobe and gently nibbled. "Taste good, too."

Molly was still warm from her shower, relaxed from sleep, pliant in his arms.

Hoot covered her mouth with his and kissed her slowly, thoroughly. He drew back just enough to look into her eyes. When she didn't resist, he kissed her again—and kept kissing her. The kisses deepened, became more urgent. Molly rose on tiptoe, wrapped her arms around his neck and pressed her body against his. Hoot cupped his hands under her hips and lifted her to align her pelvis with his erection. She wrapped her legs around him and ground her body into his. She dug her fingernails into his shoulders and moaned.

"Are you ready for some unfinished business?" he whispered against her mouth.

"Oh my God, Hoot. Oh my God."

The water stopped in the shower.

Molly clung to him, breathless. "Hoot, Let's go to your place." she whispered. "Now."

"You gonna drive or ride?"

"I'll take my car."

"I'll meet you there. Hurry." He slipped through the sliding door.

Molly grabbed a note pad and pen. She jotted, *Gil,* and stifled a giggle as she wrote, *Something came up. Had to run.*

She looked around the kitchen and shoved one coffee mug back into the cupboard. She grabbed her handbag, picked up a pair of tennis shoes by the front door and ran out of the house barefoot. She thought she saw Gil's face in the guestroom window as she backed out of the drive. She ignored a pang of guilt and sped away. She felt around in her handbag, found her cell phone and turned it off.

She skidded to a stop behind the Harley and ran up the steps onto the deck where Hoot waited. He picked her up and shoved the door open with his foot.

"Where are Emily and Oscar?" Molly asked.

"In the Ozarks." He spoke with his mouth against hers. He carried her into a room she hadn't seen on her first visit. Floor-to-ceiling windows looked out on the woods behind the house.

That was the only detail she had time to notice before he laid her on the king-size bed and ran his hands slowly over her fully clothed body. The dark pools of his eyes turned velvety soft as he gazed into hers.

His voice was husky. He said, "Babe, I'm gonna ravish you now. But that don't mean my business with you'll be done." He lifted her tee shirt, slid his hands under her back and unfastened her bra. He freed her breasts and lowered his mouth to first one, then the other. She helped him rid her of the shirt and bra.

Molly moaned and writhed under his touch as he trailed kisses down her stomach. He unbuttoned her jeans, slid the zipper down and lifted her hips to pull the jeans and panties off together. She rose halfway to help but when his mouth took over the newly exposed area, she forgot what she meant to do. She sank back on the bed and gave in to the sensation with one leg still trapped in her jeans.

She was teetering on the verge of a climax when she stopped him. "Hoot, wait. Please. Help me get my jeans off."

He rolled off the bed and pulled the jeans from her leg.

She sat up and swung her legs over the edge of the bed. She said, "Take off your clothes. I want to see you."

He pulled his black tee shirt over his head. Molly placed her hands flat against his chest and ran them lightly over his nipples. She trailed one finger along the thin line of salt and pepper hair that ran down his firm stomach and disappeared under his low-slung black jeans. He obligingly unsnapped, unzipped and stepped out of them in a smooth motion. She took him in both hands.

When Hoot reached for her, she stood and moved against him until their bodies were in contact from head to toe. He sank back on the bed and took her down on top of him.

Molly rose to her knees and mounted his erection. "Next time, you can drive," she said. Then she threw her head back and rode him home.

When it was over, they lay on their sides, gazing at each other. Hoot touched her face. "Good golly, Miss Hot Tamale!"

"I guess it's too late for me to play hard to get." Molly said. She actually was a little worried that she had come on too strong.

Hoot traced her lips with his fingers. "I wondered if you'd be a moaner or a screamer. Turns out, you're both."

"No, I'm not—I'm just—I was just—deprived." She immediately wondered how deprived Hoot had been. She wondered where he went for satisfaction, where he had gained his expertise. She wondered if he was through with her now that he had gotten what he wanted.

"How about some coffee and breakfast, Wonder Woman?" He pulled on his jeans, commando style. "You don't need to go down the hall to the bathroom you used before. There's one in here."

The master bath was spacious and clean. A large wicker basket on the floor held a stack of folded clean towels. A smaller basket on the left side of the marbled countertop held an assortment of washcloths. A half-used bar of green and white striped soap lay in a dish on the far right side. A brand new pink bar of Camay lay in the soap hollow of the sink.

Molly studied the scene before her, carefully and considerately laid out. Was it all for her? Or did Hoot keep a supply of pink bars of soap for when he had women guests? She looked at herself in the full-length mirror. What did he see in her? Her body was okay, but nothing spectacular. She was more soft than muscular. Her breasts were not as full as she would like and her hips were fuller than she would like. At least the full hips made her waist look smaller, she rationalized.

She sighed, picked a washcloth from the basket and initiated the new bar of Camay. He'd just have to come up with another bar for the next victim. By the time she had washed up and dressed, the aroma of coffee was wafting into the bedroom. She followed her nose to the kitchen and found Hoot placing a stack of French toast in the center of the island. Coffee mugs, plates, silverware, syrup and butter were already set out.

Molly watched him pour coffee and place cloth napkins on the island. He was wearing jeans and tee shirt, but was still barefoot. God, he was sexy...and talented...and smooth. And practiced? Her heart constricted at that thought.

"Do you always treat your women so nicely?" she asked. "Satisfaction guaranteed, pink soap, breakfast. Or am I special?" As soon as the words were out of her mouth, she realized how pathetic she sounded.

Hoot set the coffee pot down and came to her. He put his hands on her shoulders, looked in her eyes and said, "Molly, don't. Yes, you're special. And other women? Not sayin' there never has been, but . . ." He trailed off. "Let's eat. Then we'll talk."

She was nervous about the forthcoming talk. They ate without much conversation.

When they were finished, Molly stood and started to clear the dishes. Hoot said, "Let it go and come here." He led her into a living room with a stone fireplace and soft leather sofa and chairs. An entire wall was taken up with a built-in bookcase filled with books. Beautiful American Indian art graced the remaining walls. He sat down in an oversized leather chair and pulled her onto his lap.

"Babe, listen to me."

She closed her eyes and braced herself to have her heart broken.

His voice was a soft drawl. "Open your eyes and look at me." She did.

"Everything I'm gonna say to you is the truth. I'm never gonna lie to you."

He was silent for a moment. Then he took a deep breath and continued. "Not sure how to make you understand this, 'cause I'm not sure I understand it myself. I've always known certain things that I didn't know how I knew. But I'm as sure of them as I can be. Okay, there've been other women. But I never brought 'em here. It was just sex and I always knew I didn't want that kind of energy in my house. I knew I was saving it for the right woman." He gave an embarrassed chuckle. "I guess that sounds corny, like a virgin savin' herself for marriage. But it was one of those things I knew. And from the time I laid eyes on you in the produce department, I knew you were the one. I could tell there was music playin' in your head. I don't know how I knew, but I did. Then I was sittin' there on my bike in the parking lot thinkin' I should've done something to get your attention, when you came out of HyVee and saw your flat tire. I figured it was a sign from the universe."

"Liz thinks you slashed my tire."

"Babe, I didn't know it was your car before you came out."

"But, when you brought me here the first time, why didn't—"

"It wasn't time." He grinned. "I hadn't bought the pink soap yet."

"About the pink soap," Molly said. "What made you think to do that?"

"It's the kind I saw in your hall bathroom. I figured the other stuff might be a little rough on your sensitive parts." He ran his hand up the inside of her leg. "I've been gettin' my lair ready ever since I met you."

Molly felt like the luckiest woman on the planet. But she couldn't resist the temptation to poke at it. "Hoot, you're sexy as hell, the way you play the piano is beyond sexy, you have a great house, you can fix things and you can cook. I can't figure out what you'd want with an older woman."

His hand was doing magical things between her legs. "Babe, from what I've seen, it's a good thing you've got yourself a younger man."

"I'm serious, Hoot. I'm at least 10 pounds overweight and—"

"All soft curves, no sharp angles," he said as his fingers drove her crazy.

"And my hysterectomy scar looks like an evil grin—"

"Scar? What scar?"

"and...and I don't have a young woman's breasts. They used to be 34C but now they're more like 36 long." She was so turned on she could hardly speak.

"Good. No danger of having an eye poked out," Hoot said. He stood up and laid her on a thick rug in front of the fireplace.

"Oh, my God," Molly said, "are you going to ravish me again?"

Hoot shed his jeans and shirt and helped her undress. "You're gonna give me a big head if you don't quit callin' me God. I'm gonna make love to you. Remember, it's my turn to drive and we're goin' for a long, slow ride."

He put his hands under her hips and entered her slowly. She rose to meet him, wrapping her legs around his body.

183

"Look in my eyes, babe," he said. "Watch me while I love you." His voice was a soft caress.

Every nerve of her body was connected with every nerve of his. It was not as if he was doing something to her or she to him. Every sensation was mutual, a melding, a fusion of their bodies. Molly had heard of Tantric sex and she wondered briefly if that was what they were doing. Then her mind let go of everything except the moment.

They stayed like this for what seemed like a long time, not stroking, just concentrating on the sensations. He pulsed inside her as if seeking greater depths. She welcomed his quest with involuntary contractions that drew him in deeper. Molly had never experienced anything so erotic.

At first it was almost impossible for her to keep from closing her eyes and charging to a climax. But Hoot's soft voice kept reining her in. "Stay with me, babe. Just a little longer. Stay with me."

When she was sure she couldn't hold out another second, she begged, "Hoot, please. Now."

He obliged.

It was either the longest orgasm she'd ever experienced, or the mother of multiple orgasms.

Chapter 47

They lay entwined in each other's arms, catching their breath. Hoot drew Molly close and kissed her. "Babe, I just gave you my heart. I hope you'll take good care of it."

"That was your heart?"

"Go ahead, mock me, but—"

A phone rang. Hoot turned and looked at a combo phone and answering machine on a table by the chair they had been sitting in earlier. "I'll let the machine get it." He turned back to Molly as the ringing stopped and his recorded voice cut in, "Hoot, here. Leave a message." A beep and then:

"Hoot, this is Sophie. I'm at Mom's house where we seem to have a situation. I paged through her caller ID numbers and found yours. Would you happen to know where she is?"

Molly jumped up and grabbed the phone. "Sophie, I'm here. What's wrong?" Her heart hammered in her chest as she imagined one horror after another. Had something happened to Gus or Zach? What about Richie or Dennis? Had there been a construction accident? Had Gil set her house on fire?

"Sophie," she screamed, "talk to me. What's happened?"

"Sorry, Mom, I didn't mean to scare you. Nobody's dead or bleeding. I'm just a little surprised you answered. I mean, it's okay. I was looking for you or I wouldn't have called. But I guess I didn't really expect to find you...there."

"Sophie, if you don't stop yammering and tell me what's going on, I'll hunt you down and...and turn you over my knee."

"Mom. Calm down. Everyone's here looking for you because Gil called Richie and Dennis and told them you'd disappeared. He said you left a strange note and he was pretty sure that damned biker had something to do with it. He said he heard the bike just before you took off.

"So Richie called me, I called Liz, and everyone congregated here to read the note. But by the time we got here, Gil had gone missing, luggage and all. I hate to interrupt whatever you're doing," she cleared her throat, "but you weren't answering your cell phone, and I need you to come home and help untangle this mess. Dennis is beside himself."

"I'm on my way," Molly said. She hung up the phone and gathered her clothes. She started to step into her panties, thought better of it and headed for the bathroom with her clothes bundled in her arms.

Hoot followed her. "Babe, what can I do? What's wrong?"

"My whole family, and I'm counting Liz, have lost their friggin' minds. They're all at my house turning it into an insane asylum. Oh, yeah, and Gil's gone missing. I've got to leave." She turned at the bathroom door. "I need a minute, okay?" And she closed his own door in his face.

Molly washed, and pulled on her panties and jeans. She fastened her bra and dragged her tee shirt over her head. Every inch of her body was super sensitive. She didn't feel like hurrying and resented having to. She wondered if there was a universal law that said Molly Josephine Stark had to pay a price for a few stolen moments of pleasure. She raked her fingers through her hair and gave herself a final look in the full-length mirror. That's as good as it's going to get, she said to her reflection. If anyone doesn't like it, they can kiss my ass. Wait, no they can't. I think my ass belongs to Hoot.

He was dressed and waiting for her when she came out of the bathroom. He handed her handbag to her. She had no idea where she had left it.

"I'm followin' you home or drivin' your car," he said. "Which will it be?"

She dug her keys out and handed them to him. *Let them all think whatever they want,* she thought. Her anger was building slowly, but surely. It was all that damned Gil's fault. What right did he have to come into her home and cause all this trouble? He gets everyone riled up and then disappears. Probably hopped a plane and went back home early, like the last time.

Someone ought to push him out without a parachute while they're high over Kansas.

Chapter 48

Everyone started talking at once when Molly and Hoot walked through the door of her house.

Sophie, with raised eyebrow: "Well, you don't seem any worse for the wear."

Liz, in a gruff voice that was as close to a whisper as she could get: "Damn, I'll bet you did the deed, didn't you!"

Richie, all stiff with disapproval: "Mom, I can't imagine what you were thinking, to take off like that and worry everyone."

Dennis, to Richie: "For God's sake, Richie. She's a grown woman." And to Molly: "Mollymoms, can we sit down and talk a minute? I need to try and figure out what the old man is up to."

Molly gave everyone else a look that dared them to follow her and Dennis into the kitchen. They sat down at the table and her son-in-law began.

"You've been with Dad more than anyone else the past few days. Have you noticed any confusion, any signs of dementia? Do you think he might have wandered away and become lost?"

Her heart twisted with sympathy for Dennis, and guilt washed over her. She wrung her hands, looked away from Dennis and finally brought her eyes back to his. "I'm so sorry, Dennis. No, I don't think your dad is suffering from dementia. I think he's angry with me. Well, maybe more disappointed than angry."

She told him about Gil's infatuation with her, about the proposal and about his impatience with Hoot hanging around. "He wanted to announce our engagement at the party tomorrow. He still thinks it's a housewarming party. Dennis, I hope you find him and I'll try to help. But you can't let him make that announcement. It's not going to happen. I told him so but I'm afraid he didn't accept no for an answer."

Dennis rolled his eyes. "Well, the good news is I will not need to keep him in restraints and Depends any time soon. The bad news is—there's lots of bad news. I have to play detective and look for him. Now, tell me, do I look like a detective to you? We've got a party, people invited, food and drink being catered and no guest of honor. I'm going to find the old fart, then I'm going to kill him, then I'm going to prop his dead body up in a chair to greet people at his damned birthday party!"

He took a deep breath and managed a small smile. "Mollymoms, I suspect you have lovely news and I want to hear all about it, even if Richie is less than thrilled."

Richie ventured into the kitchen just as Dennis pulled a handkerchief from his pocket and mopped his brow. "Dennis, I heard you raising your voice and now you're sweating. What's going on?"

"Darling," Dennis said, "I don't sweat. I have the vapors."

"Well, you're working up a glisten," Richie said.

Molly noticed everyone had surged into the kitchen behind Richie and they all seemed to be waiting expectantly for the next move.

"I suppose we need to get organized and make a plan," Dennis said. "I don't think it's been long enough to report him missing."

"Does he know anyone else around here?" Hoot asked.

Liz slapped her forehead. "Good thinking, biker boy. Dennis, before you get your tidy whities in a wad, someone ought to call the wicked witch of the Midwest. I wouldn't put it past her to abduct him, drug him and have him on a cruise ship halfway to the Cayman Islands by the time he wakes up."

There were snorts and giggles all around—probably everyone remembering the spectacle of Jan eating meatballs and spaghetti in front of Gil—but Molly thought it was worth checking out.

She took the phone off the wall and dialed Jan's house. There was no answer. She tried her cell next. Jan answered, "Hello, Molly, is that you?"

"Yes it is, Jan. Can I speak to Gil, please?"

There was a long silence, then, "What makes you think he's with me?"

"Liz had a hunch, Jan. And I'm learning to respect hunches." She caught Hoot's eye and he grinned.

"Why are you so interested in his whereabouts now?" Jan asked. "I understand everyone took off and left him all alone this morning. It's a good thing he has me to fall back on."

"Listen, Jan. He has everyone wringing hands and thinking something awful has happened to him. Dennis is worried sick. Now put him on the damned phone."

There was some muffled conversation and Gil's voice came on. "Molly, I'm sorry if—"

"Gil, just a minute. Here's Dennis."

Dennis took the phone. "Dad, whatever were you thinking to take off like...Wait. Let me start over." He put his hand over the mouthpiece and looked at Richie. "Sorry, pot to kettle," he said. Then speaking into the phone again, "Dad, come on back. We need to talk."

Dennis was silent, listening. "I see. You *will* be at the party tomorrow, won't you? After all, it was pretty much your idea."

Another silence. "Oh, she did, huh. Well, then you understand how important it is that you show up. Okay, I'll see you tomorrow. Shall I pick you up? She will? Fine. Tomorrow then."

Dennis disconnected and handed the phone to Molly. He scanned the curious faces and said, "He's decided to stay at Jan's for the rest of his visit. She'll bring him to the party tomorrow—and it's no longer a surprise party. Jan blabbed, allegedly to keep him from taking an early flight home. I'm relieved to find him, but the phrase unholy alliance keeps running through my head."

The small crowd began to disperse. Molly thought the mood seemed anticlimactic, as if they had all been ready to pin on deputy badges and ride off to search for Gil. Now they didn't know what to do with themselves. Sad, sad. Didn't these people have a life? But then, maybe she was just feeling smug because her life had taken such an exciting turn.

190

As they headed out, Dennis turned to Hoot and offered his hand. "Thanks for your input. And please know you're invited to the party if you're brave enough or crazy enough to further your involvement with this nutty family."

Richie's head snapped around and he opened his mouth, but Dennis squeezed his shoulder and herded him through the door.

Hoot draped his arm around Molly as they watched everyone leave. "Babe, I'll never have a dull moment now that you're my woman. You are my woman, aren't you?"

"I'm a little worried that you seem to fit in so well with my nutty family. It makes me wonder what's wrong with you. But to answer your question, yes, I'm your woman."

She was relieved when Hoot asked her to take him back to his house. He said there were a couple of things he needed to take care of. For her part, Molly wanted to be alone for a while and process the last few hours. They agreed he would be back to accompany her to the party tomorrow.

~~

It wasn't unusual for Molly to dream about Sam. In her dreams, he was out of reach, but just barely. She would move toward him and sometimes he would allow her to touch him. Always, he smiled at her with love in his eyes.

This dream started out the same but took a disturbing turn. When Molly reached for him, he turned and walked away. She called after him but he disappeared into the mist. She tried to follow but was soon lost and alone in the mist. She awoke, heart racing, her face wet with tears. She lay there until morning, her mind shifting between images of Sam and Hoot.

~~

Molly called Hoot and asked if he could come a little early before time to leave for the party.

"Is anything wrong, babe?"

"No, well yes, well...I don't know. I just need to talk."

"I'll be there in 15 minutes."

Molly opened the door and stared, open-mouthed, at the man who stood in front of her. He wore gray slacks with a slender black leather belt, a burgundy striped Oxford shirt, a gray tie with a subtle burgundy pattern and black loafers. But

191

the most amazing thing about his appearance was that his hair was cropped short and neat. It wasn't exactly a crew cut, but close. It was Hoot, all right, but a version of him that she hadn't seen before and couldn't have imagined. And he was breathtakingly gorgeous.

Molly reached up to touch the back of his head. "What did you do with it?"

"I cut it off, put it in a baggie and mailed it to Locks of Love. It finally got long enough, 10 inches, so it was time."

"Some of the guys where I used to work grew their hair for that cause. But I thought they only made wigs for children. What about the gray in your hair?"

"I've been donatin' my hair since before there was gray in it. And they still want it. They sell it to offset manufacturing costs. I hope that wasn't the only reason you were attracted to me."

Molly stepped back and studied him. "It's a new look, but I think I can get used to it," she understated. "And you're all dressed up. You'll probably be the best dressed guy at the party."

"I doubt it, considerin' there's gonna be at least a couple of gay guys there. And speakin' of all dressed up..." He gave her the head-to-toe-once- over, taking in every detail. She wore a soft black pantsuit accented with a belt made of silver circles linked together. Her silver earrings matched the circles in the belt. Strappy silver flats completed the ensemble. Her look was simple, yet elegant. "You look good enough to eat," he said.

"As do you," she said, stepping into his arms. He kissed her, and then held her at arm's length.

"Babe, if we're gonna make it to the party, we better stop now. And what did you want to talk to me about?"

She sat on the sofa and motioned for him to sit beside her. "I had this dream," she said. "I don't know what it meant, but I can't get it out of my head." She told him about the dream and how it was different from her usual dreams about Sam.

Hoot listened without speaking until she was finished. Then he took her hands in his and looked into her eyes.

"Molly, I know you loved Sam. And that's okay with me. And I want you to know I'll never try to take his place. I just want to have a place of my own in your life.

"I can't say what the dream meant. That's for you to figure out. But if you can communicate with Sam's spirit — and I believe it's possible, you can assure him I'll always respect your memories of him. And ask him to let you love me 'cause I'll treasure you and take care of you."

They sat there in silence, Molly's hands in Hoot's, for several minutes. And then a strange thing happened. Sam had brought her some tiny wind chimes from a business trip to Arizona. She had hung them from the ceiling in front of the picture window where they caught light but no breeze. And now they tinkled ever so slightly. She turned her head to look at them. Hoot followed her gaze. A peaceful feeling descended on her.

Chapter 49

On the way to the party, Molly asked Hoot, "Am I going to have to get used to spooky, woohoo things happening now that you're in my life?"

He smiled at her. "They happen all the time to everyone. People don't usually notice. But now that you're gonna be gettin' regular Hoot injections, you'll prob'ly start noticin' more."

Molly thought about that. Psychic by osmosis? She supposed she could handle the psychic part and she was sure she could handle the osmosis process.

Hoot's cell phone rang. He plucked it off his belt and answered. "This is Hoot." He listened for what seemed like a long time. Then, "Where is she now? Which hospital? I'm on my way.

"Babe," he turned to Molly. "I'm gonna have to bail on you. Take me back to my bike. I'll catch up with you as soon as...well, I don't know. As soon as I can." He avoided her eyes and stared at his cell phone, still in his hand.

Molly whipped the car around at Kentucky and Courtney, her heart pounding. "Is it Emily?" she asked.

"No, not Emily." After a moment he continued, barely above a whisper, "It's Estelle."

Who the hell was Estelle? Neither of them spoke until Molly pulled into her driveway. She turned to him. He had his hand on the door handle.

"Who is Estelle?"

"Babe, I'm sorry. I don't have time to explain right now. I'll call you." And he was gone.

He roared out of the driveway on his bike and left her sitting there, all dressed up with no place to go. How could he do this to her? No explanation. After the grand speech about how he would treasure her and take care of her. After he swore he would never lie to her. Well he hadn't lied, exactly. But it seemed like he'd done a hell of a job of omitting. She got out, slammed the door shut with her right foot and gave it a vicious kick with her left.

"Ouch, damn, fuck, son-of-a-bitch." A voice in her head told her she shouldn't have done that in open-toed sandals. Besides, Hoot wasn't there to hear her talk dirty...Hoot, the miserable, secretive, son of...oh, shit, her toe hurt! And so did her broken heart.

When she put her weight on her left foot, the pain made her gasp. She hobbled up the steps, foot turned to the side, keeping the weight off her big toe. She went inside and picked up the phone. Liz didn't answer. Of course not. Liz was at the party. Where Molly was supposed to be. Where Hoot was supposed to be. With Molly.

She fought back tears. She was too damned mad to cry. She'd go to the party and dance with another man. Well maybe not dance. Her big toe was throbbing. Besides the only available straight man she could expect to see at this party was no longer available. Jan had snatched him up.

Was it too late to win him back? Why would she want to? What was wrong with her? What she wanted was the man who had just deserted her to rush to Estelle. Who the HELL was Estelle?

Chapter 50

The first thing she saw when got to the party was Gil and Jan dancing cheek to cheek. Jan looked ecstatic. Gil looked bemused. Molly remembered how it felt to dance with Gil. She dropped her sequined clutch onto the nearest table and marched, well limped, up to them. She tapped Jan on the shoulder.

"Cutting in, Jan."

Jan gave her a look that would have killed a weaker woman. Gil dropped his arms away from Jan and turned to Molly. They began to move to the music. Molly tried to ignore the pain in her toe and moved in close to Gil. She concentrated on how it felt to be in his arms again. He was big, tall and solid.

She felt small, protected—

"Where have you been, darling? I was about to give up on you. Have you changed your mind?"

She felt engulfed, smothered.

She thought of how she felt in Hoot's arms. What happened to that? Molly stopped dancing and began to sob. *It wasn't about Hoot*, she told herself. Her toe hurt like hell. "I'm sorry, Gil. I think I've got a broken toe."

Gil helped her to a chair at a table where Joe sat watching Liz do the bus stop with a guy in a flaming pink shirt and skintight leather pants.

Joe glanced at Molly and said, "I know she ain't right, but you gotta love her, don't you." Then he really looked at Molly and his eyes got big. "Oh, shit. What's wrong, hon?"

"My toe," Molly whimpered. She raised her foot to show him. He took her foot in his hand and eased her sandal off.

"Liz," he yelled. "Come here."

The next instant, Liz was there taking in the scene. "My God, Gil. Did you stomp on her toe? No, I'll bet it was Jan."

"It wasn't either one," Molly said. "I hurt it on my car door."

Liz narrowed her eyes. "Where's Hoot? Molly, did you kick the car door? You did, didn't you? Joe, carry her into one of the bedrooms. I want to talk to her."

Gil watched the proceedings with his hands hanging at his sides, palms up, an ineffectual "what now?" look on his face. Jan sidled up to him and draped one of his arms over her shoulder.

~~

"So, he's never mentioned any Estelle before?" Liz asked.

"Never," Molly said. She lay on a bed in the guestroom with her foot propped up on two pillows. Most everyone had been banished from the room and ordered to resume partying. Only Liz and Dennis were presently in the room with her.

Dennis stopped pacing and faced Molly with his arms crossed. "Mollymoms, I say you fight for your man," he said as Richie came through the door with a bag of ice.

"It can't be much of a fight, Mom," Richie said. "I don't think Gil is that crazy about Aunt Jan."

"Wrong man, wrong other woman, darling," Dennis said. "We'll talk later. Right now, somebody needs to go to the emergency room and get her toe x-rayed."

"I'm taking her," Liz said. "You all get back in there with your guests. Gil hasn't opened his birthday presents yet. Molly, we'll take your car. Joe can come after me when I get you home."

~~

Turn right on Kentucky," Molly ordered as Liz barreled south on 291."

"What the hell for?"

"I want to talk to Little Em."

"What if Hoot and his honey are there?"

"I'll kill them. Have you got a gun on you?"

Liz turned on Kentucky. "People are going to be reading about us in the paper tomorrow," she complained. But she followed Molly's directions and turned onto the gravel lane. Emily came out of the little house and peered at the car. Her face lit up when she recognized Molly. She bustled up to the passenger door.

"Hi, Molly. I haven't seen you for a while. Who's your friend? Come on in, both of you. I'll put on a fresh pot of coffee."

"Emily, this is my best friend, Liz. Liz, this is Hoot's Aunt Emily. He calls her Little Em," she said, fighting to keep her voice from cracking along with her heart.

"Emily, I'm sorry to drop in on you like this, but I need to ask you a question. Who is Estelle?"

Emily searched Molly's tear-stained face. She pursed her lips and spat out the name. "Estelle. Estelle Emery. Why do you ask?"

Molly told her about the phone call and Hoot's sudden departure. Emily shook her head. "I thought Hoot was done with that years ago."

"But who is she?" Molly asked.

"Estelle and her husband, Scooter, used to have a bar out on the highway. She tried to keep it going while he was in the Army back in the '60s or '70s. I heard Scooter died a few years ago. Any more than that, honey, you'll have to ask Hoot." She looked past Molly and said, "It was nice to meet you, Liz." Then she turned and ambled away.

"The plot thickens," Liz said. And then she drove a pain-wracked Molly to the emergency room. But only a small part of the pain emanated from her toe.

Chapter 51

Three hours and 47 minutes later, Molly was handed off to Liz with an ugly blue post-op shoe on her left foot and a strappy silver sandal on her right foot. The left sandal was in her lap.

"Sorry it took so long," a nurse told her, as she pushed Molly in a wheelchair. "Things are always total chaos on a Saturday night in Emergency."

"I can see you're busy," Liz said. "You go on back to work. I'll take it from here." She shoved the nurse aside and had Molly down a hall and around a corner before the nurse could react. She hit a handicap-activated button on a ladies' room door and pushed Molly through. After a moment, she peeked out the door and announced, "All clear."

"Liz, what the hell are you doing?" Molly asked.

"Okay, listen up. While you've been lying around nursing your toe, I've been busy. I know what room Estelle is in. And I saw Hoot. I told him you were here with a broken toe. I told him I thought he should come and see about you."

"Oh, God, Liz. You didn't."

"Damn straight, I did."

Molly's small sequined handbag buzzed in her lap. She fished out her cell phone. "Hello."

"Molly, it's Hoot. I ran into Liz in the hall. She told me what happened. Are you all right? Where are you?"

"Like you care. You'd better get back to Estelle, whoever the hell she is."

She heard him take a deep breath and blow it out. "Meet me in the chapel and talk to me."

"I'm not exactly mobile. Liz is pushing me around in a wheelchair."

"Let me talk to her."

199

Molly handed the phone to Liz. "He wants to talk to you."

Liz took the phone. "Yeah?"

She listened for a moment, disconnected and backed Molly out of the ladies' room.

By the time Molly realized where Liz was taking her, they were at the hospital chapel and Hoot stood at the door. He held it open while Liz wheeled her inside. "I'll be back in 15 minutes," she said and turned and left.

Hoot looked like hell. His tie hung loose around his neck and the top two buttons of his shirt were undone. Molly said, "You look like hell. Who is this damned woman, Estelle, and what is she to you?"

Hoot set the brakes on the wheelchair and knelt in front of her. "Estelle's an old friend. She's very dear to me. It doesn't change anything between you and me."

"Like hell, it doesn't." Molly yanked the wheels in a futile attempt to move the wheelchair. It didn't budge.

"Molly," Hoot said, "I want to explain, but I've got to get back." He reached out to touch her face. She jerked her head away.

"Go on then. It's the second time tonight you've chosen her over me."

"Babe, you've got a broken toe. Estelle's dyin'. " He rose from his knees and walked out of the chapel.

Molly couldn't remember when she had felt more abandoned as she sat and waited for Liz. She knew Liz wouldn't be back until the full 15 minutes had passed. Tears flowed from her eyes, rolled down her face and splashed onto her useless party finery.

Ten minutes later, Liz barged through the door bristling with excitement. "Molly," she said, "you're not going to believe this." She maneuvered the wheelchair through the doorway and into the hall, talking non-stop. "I got a good look at Estelle. She looks like 20 miles of bad road."

"Well, Liz, she is dying, so I hear. How would you expect her to look?"

"That's not what I mean. She's...wait here. I'm going to get the car." She parked the wheelchair just inside the entrance to the emergency room and flew through the doors.

Did she really think it was necessary to tell me to wait here? Molly wondered. God, she felt grumpy.

Liz was back in record time. She pushed the wheelchair out to the car, helped Molly in, slammed the door and gave the wheelchair a shove in the general direction of the doors they had just come through. Then she ran around to driver's side, jumped in and took off.

"Anyhow, that's not what I mean," she continued as if there hadn't been a break in the conversation. "She looks old. Really old. And this just keeps getting stranger. When I walked in and stood looking at her, she opened her eyes and croaked out, 'Are you Molly?' I said no and turned around to leave. A nurse passed me coming in as I was going out. She looked at me and shook her head, kind of sad, and I beat it out of there. I'm telling you, weird clings to Hoot like ugly on an ape. We should keep away from him before we get sucked into some alternate universe or something. He's spooky!"

"Liz, was he in the room when this happened?"

"No. I wouldn't have gone in there if he had been. I thought he was with you."

"He didn't stay with me very long. I do wonder why Estelle would ask if you're me. Maybe it's some other Molly she's looking for. But my point is, if Hoot wasn't in the room, what makes you think he has anything to do with it?"

Remember how he did the psychic thing at 54th Street Grill? And he just stands around all quiet and looking like he knows something the rest of us don't. I'm telling you, he's spooky."

"Can we talk about this tomorrow, Liz? I'm so tired. They gave me something for pain and I'm about to fall asleep sitting up."

"Fine." She dug her cell phone out of her handbag, punched a number and barked, "Joe, meet me at Molly's. I'm gonna need help getting her drugged up ass in the house."

Chapter 52

It was the third day off the pain medication and her head had finally ceased feeling like it was full of cotton. When the phone rang, she recognized Hoot's cell phone number. She picked up and said, "What?"

"Molly. Babe. Why do you sound so angry?"

"What do you want?"

"I'm goin' home to shower and change clothes, and catch a couple hours of sleep. Can I come by and see you before I go back?"

"Go back where?" She knew where but she asked anyway.

"Back to the hospital."

"I'm surprised you can spare the time." She was sure she sounded as bitchy as she felt.

"Babe, if you saw Estelle, you wouldn't think whatever it is you're thinkin'. Let me come over. Say 3 o'clock. Give me a chance to explain." He sounded exhausted.

"Call first." She hung up.

Three o'clock. Two and a half hours from now. An idea was forming in her mind. She looked up the number for patient information at the hospital.

~~

Forty minutes later, she stood at the door of Estelle's room and peeked in. All she could see was a mass of long, wavy platinum blonde hair spread on the pillow. The woman's face was turned toward the window. Molly watched for a few minutes until she decided Estelle was asleep, and then she limped to the foot of the bed as quietly as she could. It wasn't easy to skulk with one foot encased in a clumsy blue shoe with a rigid sole.

The woman lying in the bed was wrinkled and wasted. Molly realized the hair was gray rather than blonde. She flashed back to a long-ago Dick Tracy comic where Gravel Gertie went to college. The young studs, seeing her from behind with her slender figure and flowing platinum hair, would move in on her, and then be shocked when they saw her wrinkled old face.

Estelle opened her eyes and slowly focused on Molly. Those faded blue eyes, too big in her emaciated face, had the look of death, which Molly recognized from Sam's final days.

"Oh, I...I'm sorry," Molly stammered. "I must be in the wrong room." She turned to go.

"Wait." Estelle's voice was stronger than her appearance warranted. "Are you Molly?"

It was the last thing Molly expected to hear. She turned back, hobbled to the bedside and looked down at Estelle. "How did you know?"

"I'm dying, I'm not dumb. All my senses are heightened." She took a ragged breath. "Hoot told me about you." She closed her eyes and seemed to be resting.

Molly had almost decided to slip out of the room when Estelle opened her eyes and began to speak. "Do you remember *The Graduate?*"

"The movie? Yes, but why...?"

Estelle coughed, a long, wracking cough that shook her frail body. Finally she said, "I was Hoot's Mrs. Robinson."

Dear God, how old was this woman? Molly was sure she hadn't spoken out loud, but Estelle rasped, "Seventy-seven. I was 40, he was 21."

Coo-coo ca-choo, Mrs. Robinson played in Molly's mind while Anne Bancroft seduced Dustin Hoffman. The image morphed into one of Hoot and the ghastly creature in the hospital bed. She shook her head to dislodge the mental picture.

"I was a knockout then," Estelle mumbled. Her faded eyes filled with tears. "God, I loved him." She raised a shaking hand and brushed at the tears. "But I had to let him go. I hope you know how lucky you are."

Molly felt tears slide down her own face. She didn't know if the tears were for this shell of a woman or for herself.

Estelle's face was a study in pain, how much was physical and how much emotional, Molly couldn't guess. She awkwardly took the woman's cold hand. Estelle's dry lips stretched in what was probably meant to be a smile. "Run along now." She pulled her hand away from Molly's, the smile faded and she closed her eyes. "Don't hurt him."

~~

When she got back home, there was a message from Hoot on her answering machine. He said he wouldn't be coming by after all. The hospital had called. Estelle had taken a turn for the worse and was asking for him.

Chapter 53

Molly sat at the kitchen table and sipped coffee while she waited for the sun to rise and the day to unfold. It was forecast to be another July scorcher and the itchy post-op shoe served to add to her misery. While she was on the subject of misery, she thought about Hoot. She hadn't heard from him since he left the message on her answering machine saying he'd been called back to the hospital. Not a single word. That was four days ago.

She had picked up the phone several times, intending to call him, but then hanging up without dialing. She didn't know what she would say. She didn't know if she would be intruding. She didn't know what the situation was. Had Estelle died? Was Hoot still sitting by her bedside?

She heard an alarm go off in the guestroom and her thoughts turned to Gil.

Jan had brought him to Molly's house late yesterday afternoon. She'd called from her cell phone. "Molly, open the door. I'm dropping Gil off. He wants to come back to your house. And that's fine with me. The man doesn't even have a passport! You can take him to the airport tomorrow." She'd disconnected without another word.

Molly had looked out in time to see Jan speed away. Gil stood in the driveway with his luggage, looking forlorn.

Now she waited for Gil to get dressed and join her in the kitchen. She heard him emerge from the guestroom and go into the bathroom down the hall, whistling. Her mind bounced back to Hoot while she listened to the sound of water running in the guest shower—and imagined the roar of a motorcycle.

There was a light tap on the deck door. Molly got up and pulled back the blinds. Hoot stood there. She wondered for a

205

moment if she had conjured him. She unlocked the door and opened it a crack. "What do you want?"

"I want to talk to you. And some coffee would be nice." Hoot slid the door open and came inside.

Molly pointed to the extra mug she had put out for Gil, and then sat back down. "You'll have to talk fast. I'm leaving for the airport in 20 minutes."

Hoot helped himself to a mug of coffee. "The airport?" When Molly didn't answer, he sat in the chair next to her and waited. After a moment, he looked at her foot, encased in the blue shoe. "Sorry about your toe. Guess I owe you a dance when it heals."

That isn't what hurts," Molly said. "And what you owe me is an explanation."

Pipes squeaked and the sound of running water ceased. Doors opened and closed.

Hoot raised an eyebrow. "Company?"

"Gil's here."

"Oh."

"And you may as well know I went to see Estelle. You asked to come and see me to explain four days ago, then you cancelled and I didn't hear another word from you. I don't know what you could say to me now that would make everything right."

"Babe, I'm sorry I didn't tell you about her. I'm sorry I hurt you and I want to make things right."

"Oh, you hurt me all right. You hurt me a lot." Molly felt the hurt fill her eyes and run down her cheeks. "First you deserted me with no explanation on the way to the party, because Estelle was in the hospital. A few hours later, you didn't have time for me when I was hurting in the same hospital. Then you said you'd come by four days ago, but you left a message and cancelled. I didn't hear a word from you during those four days. Not so much as a phone call." She knew she sounded petulant and childish, but she couldn't stop. "It's been all about Estelle, all the time."

Hoot backed his chair away from Molly. "Sounds to me like you want it to be all about Molly, all the time. Woman, you've got a mean, selfish streak a mile wide. You say you saw her. Didn't you feel anything besides sorry for yourself? How can you fault me for bein' with an old friend who would've died alone if I hadn't been there? You're comparin' a broken toe and a missed party to someone dyin'."

Molly gasped. *What was wrong with him?* She was the injured party here. *Wasn't she?*

Hoot took a breath and continued. "I came here this morning to tell you everything about me and Estelle that I couldn't tell you before because of a promise I made years ago. But Estelle set me free from that promise before she died and now you're actin' like a spoiled brat."

Still smarting from his words, Molly picked up her mug, looked into and set it back down without drinking.

"You'll never be free of her," Molly said.

Hoot stood and pushed his chair back under the table.

"I guess you're right. She was a big part of my life at one time. I can't change that, wouldn't if I could, and it seems like you can't accept it."

Gil chose that moment to stroll into the kitchen and drop a duffle bag on the floor. His hair was damp from the shower.

"I didn't expect to see you here, Holcombe," he said. "What's going on?"

Hoot barely glanced at him.

"I see you got a haircut," Gil continued. "Did you lose your strength along with the braid? You know, like Samson?"

Molly could almost feel Gil bristling with aggression.

Hoot took a step toward Gil. "I understood the reference and I can still kick your ass."

Apparently Gil wasn't the only one feeling aggressive. Molly moved between them. "Gil, we need to leave. Is the luggage in the car?"

"All but my duffle bag. I'll wait in the car, darling. Don't be long." He picked up his duffle bag, left the kitchen quickly and slammed the front door behind him.

"So it's 'darling' now?" Hoot looked pained. It's only been four days. It didn't take you long to move him back in."

"It was a long four days," Molly snapped. "You told me once you had your heart broken a long time ago. Now I know who broke it and I'm not interested in competing with a memory."

Hoot opened his arms and took a step toward her. "Molly, don't do this."

She wanted to let him hold her but she couldn't. She wanted to hurt him. Mostly, she wanted to take away his power to hurt her. She heard herself say, "My mind's made up. Just go!"

His arms dropped to his sides, his shoulders slumped and he blew out a long, slow breath.

"I guess there's nothin' left to say...except you're not the woman I thought I knew." He turned and went out the sliding door.

She didn't move until the sound of his bike faded. Then she locked the door and limped out to her car where Gil waited.

Chapter 54

"How does it feel to be rid of the ugly blue shoe?" Liz asked.

"A big relief. I never want to lay eyes on it again."

They sat in Liz's kitchen on a sunny Saturday morning in October. Molly drank coffee and ignored the plate of scones Liz had just set on the table. "I know they're not up to Little Em's standards," Liz said, as she took a bite of one, "but this is only my third batch."

Joe came through the garage door into the kitchen with a package of lawn bags under his arm. "Hi, Molly. What do you think about this woman of mine—learning to make scones!" He hugged Liz with his free arm, nuzzled her neck, gave her a loud smack on the lips and reached for a scone.

Liz patted him on the rear and threw a sultry look over her shoulder. "Later, sweet cakes. You don't get your ashes hauled until you haul the leaves out of my gutters. Besides, we've got company."

Joe left the kitchen with his lawn bags and his scone.

Liz turned her attention back to Molly. "Now that your foot's healed, how's the broken heart?"

"It sure as hell doesn't help to sit here and be reminded of Little Em, and scones, and gutters that need cleaning. And if that isn't enough, I get to watch you two lovebirds play grab ass before I go home to an empty house and dirty gutters." She pushed her chair back and started to stand.

"Molly Josephine Stark," Liz narrowed her eyes, "just plant your ass right back in that chair and listen to me for a minute. You've been moping around in a blue funk for three months, feeling sorry for yourself. And I'm getting a little tired of it. Your pain is self-inflicted. I understand why you turned Gil down. But I've always had a little trouble understanding

209

why Hoot's loyalty to a poor dying woman—who obviously still loved him—was such a bad thing. I can't believe I'm taking up for the biker, but I'd say that kind of loyalty to an old friend goes in the good column."

"What about the fact that he left me alone all this time with a broken toe? Why are you suddenly on his side?"

"For God's sake, Molly. He left you alone because you ran him off! Get over yourself!"

Molly fought back tears. "Oh, Liz. He's just too much—too much of everything. Too gorgeous, too talented, too good at everything he does. And too young. What happens when I start looking old before he does?"

Liz reached across the table and took Molly's hand. "I never told you this, but I almost let Joe get away because I was afraid I couldn't hold onto him. He was such a jock. Other girls were always flirting with him. Yeah, I was little and cute then, but I was already beginning to fight my weight.

"Then one day I decided I'd rather settle for as many years as I could keep him than not have him at all. And look at us now, more than 40 years later. He still loves me—every chubby inch of me."

~~

A half hour later, Molly was on her way home, thinking about Liz and Joe. She'd never had an inkling back then about Liz's misgivings.

She turned on the car radio as she crossed the Missouri River and continued south on 291. Janet Joplin was belting out "Me and Bobby McGee." It made her wonder, how many tomorrows would she trade for a single yesterday when Hoot made love to her? Damn! Was the universe trying to tell her something? She remembered when Hoot had said "spooky, woohoo" things happen all the time to everyone but people don't usually notice. Well, so what? It's too late now. She snapped the radio off.

As she coasted down the long hill toward Courtney Road and slowed for the right turn. Her attention was drawn to a beat-up green truck on the shoulder of the northbound lanes. The top half of the man was busy under the raised hood. She could just make out "Big O" on the battered door. My God, that's Oscar's truck, she realized.

She started to complete the turn onto Courtney. No, she couldn't do that. Oscar was a good guy and he couldn't help who his nephew was. He might walk like Hoot and talk like Hoot, but she'd bet anything he didn't carry a cell phone like Hoot. She couldn't leave him on the side of the road with engine trouble. She changed lanes again, made a U-turn at Kentucky Road and drove back to the truck. She pulled in behind it, got out of her car and slammed the door.

"Need some help, Oscar?" she yelled.

"Don't know what you could do," the muffled voice answered. "The battery's dead as doornail."

"I could give you a jump-start."

Hoot's head came out from under the hood. "I'll bet you could." He looked her up and down in that disturbing way he had.

"Or...or a lift," she stammered. "I didn't expect to see you. I thought it was Oscar."

"And I didn't expect to see you. I figured you'd be in Colorado with Gil."

"Not in a million years. We've agreed to get along for the boys' sake. But that's all it will ever be. Now, how about that lift?"

"Thanks, but I don't want to trouble you. I can walk. It's not that far."

She lowered her sunglasses just enough to look over them. "You could do that. Or I could get you home before your ice cream melts."

Hoot grinned. His teeth flashed white in his grease-smudged face. "What makes you think I'm not waitin' for someone else to get me?"

There were so many questions she wanted to ask: Why do you have Oscar's truck? Where's your bike? How've you been? Are you over Estelle? Do you miss me?

Instead she summoned her courage and asked, "Are you, Hoot? Waiting for someone else?"

"Goddamnit, Molly, I've been waitin' for you—for three months. No, all my life."

211

The universe wasn't just trying to tell her something. It was smacking her upside the head. "I'm here, now. Is it too late?" She took a step toward him.

He let out a whoop, picked her up, swung her around, and set her down. "Babe, I'm about to get you all dirty."

"And I'm about to give you a jump-start."

Molly knew there would be long talks ahead, hurts to be mended on both sides. But all of that could wait. She was in Hoot's arms, and nothing else mattered.

He pulled back and searched her face. "Where do we go from here, Molly?"

"How about your place? It's closer than mine." He grinned. "Then what?"

She pressed her body against his and made a brazen suggestion.

"God, I love it when you talk dirty," he said.

Molly broke the speed limit on the way to Hoot's Roost.

47958482R10124

Made in the USA
San Bernardino, CA
13 April 2017